Volume **7** # THE GOLDEN BOOK ENCYCLOPEDIA

fable to furniture

fa-fu

An exciting, up-to-date encyclopedia
in 20 fact-filled, entertaining volumes

Especially designed as
a first encyclopedia for
today's grade-school children

More than 2,500 full-color
photographs and illustrations

From the Publishers of Golden® Books

Western Publishing Company, Inc.
Racine, Wisconsin 53404

ILLUSTRATION CREDITS
(t=top, b=bottom, c=center, l=left, r=right)

1 l. Dennis O'Brien/Joseph, Mindlin & Mulvey; 1 r. Turi MacCombie/Evelyne Johnson Associates; 3 bl. Illustration from *Golden Treasury of Children's Literature*, © 1966 Western Publishing Company, Inc.; 4. From *The Giant Golden Book of Elves and Fairies*, illustrated by Garth Williams, © 1951 Western Publishing Company, Inc.; 5 tl. Illustration from *Grimm's Fairy Tales*, © 1986 Richard Walz, used by permission of Western Publishing Company, Inc.; 5 tr. Illustration copyright © 1983 by Trina Schart Hyman, all rights reserved, reprinted from *Little Red Riding Hood* by permission of Holiday House; 6–7, Marcus Hamilton; 8 tl, Blair Seitz/Photo Researchers; 9, Junebug Clark/Photo Researchers; 10–11 t, Gary Lippincott/Publishers' Graphics; 10 b, U.S. Department of Agriculture; 12, Jan Halaska/Photo Researchers; 13, © Joe Viesti; 14 tr, Allen Green/Photo Researchers; 14 cr, New York Public Library Picture Collection; 14 b, Joe Munroe/Photo Researchers; 15 tl, Allen Green/Photo Researchers; 15 b, B. Krueger/Photo Researchers; 16–17 and 17 br, Jane Kendall/Publishers' Graphics; 18 bl, Michael O'Reilly/Joseph, Mindlin & Mulvey; 19 tl, Confederation Life Collection; 19 cr, David Lindroth Inc.; 20 tl, Chuck O'Rear/Woodfin Camp; 21 insets b, Tanya Rebelo/Joseph, Mindlin & Mulvey; 22–23, Gary Lippincott/Publishers' Graphics; 24 both, U.S. Air Force; 25 t, Brad Hamann; 26 all, Jane Burton/Bruce Coleman Inc.; 27, Jim Amos/Photo Researchers; 28 cl, Bill Gallery/Stock, Boston; 28 br, © Joe Viesti; 29 tl, H. Armstrong Roberts; 29 br, Joe Rychetnik/Photo Researchers; 30–31, Tom Powers/Joseph, Mindlin & Mulvey; 32 tl, Lloyd P. Birmingham; 32 br and 33 cl, Dennis O'Brien/Joseph, Mindlin & Mulvey; 33 b, Mei-Ku Huang, M.D./Evelyne Johnson Associates; 34–35, Frank Mayo; 36–37 b and 38–39 b, John Rice/Joseph, Mindlin & Mulvey; 39 tl, Steve Solum/Bruce Coleman Inc.; 40 tl, Carl Roessler/Bruce Coleman Inc.; 40 b, Chris Newbert/Bruce Coleman Inc.; 41, Ken Levinson; 42–43 t, Kal Muller/Woodfin Camp; 42 bl, Jim Brandenburg/Woodfin Camp; 42 inset br, John Rice/Joseph, Mindlin & Mulvey; 44 cl, David Lindroth Inc.; 44–45 c, David Lindroth Inc.; 45 t, George A. Gabriel; 45 br, Lloyd P. Birmingham; 46 b, John Giannini/Gamma-Liaison; 47 tl, Massachusetts Department of Commerce and Development, Division of Tourism; 48–49 c, Florida Department of Commerce, Division of Tourism; 49 tr, Marilyn Bass; 50, Lloyd P. Birmingham; 51 tl, Turi MacCombie/Evelyne Johnson Associates; 51 br, Norman Owen Tomalin/Bruce Coleman Inc.; 52, Richard Hutchings; 53 bl, William McPherson/Bruce Coleman Inc.; 53 inset, Bob Gossington/Bruce Coleman Inc.; 54–55 b, Turi MacCombie/Evelyne Johnson Associates; 55 t, Marilyn Bass; 55 br, E.R. Degginger/Bruce Coleman Inc.; 56 bl, Dennis O'Brien/Joseph, Mindlin & Mulvey; 56 br, Kim Taylor/Bruce Coleman Inc.; 57 t, © Joe Viesti; 57 inset, Lloyd P. Birmingham; 58, © Joe Viesti; 59, Lowell Georgia/Photo Researchers; 60, Sandy Rabinowitz/Publishers' Graphics; 61 t, Juan Barberis/Melissa Turk & The Artist Network; 62 tr, Margot Granitsas/Photo Researchers; 62 bl, Michael O'Reilly/Joseph, Mindlin & Mulvey; 63–65 all , Fiona Reid/Melissa Turk & The Artist Network; 66 tl, Mei-Ku Huang, M.D./Evelyne Johnson Associates; 66 tr, Peter Menzel/Stock, Boston; 67 t, Ron Sherman/Bruce Coleman Inc.; 68 b, David Lindroth Inc.; 69 tr, Robert Frank/Melissa Turk & The Artist Network; 69 b, Focus on Sports; 70, Courtesy Gerald R. Ford Library; 71 b, Bettmann Archive; 71 inset, Ford Motor Company; 72–73, David Madison/Bruce Coleman Inc.; 73 inset, Tom Myers/California Office of Tourism; 74, Swiss National Tourist Office; 75, Leonard Lee Rue III/Bruce Coleman Inc.; 76 bl, F. Gohier/Photo Researchers; 78, New York Convention and Visitors Bureau; 79 tr, David Lindroth Inc.; 79 bl, Leonard Lee Rue III/National Audubon Society/Photo Researchers; 80, © Joe Viesti; 82–83, Gary Lippincott/Publishers' Graphics; 84 bl, David Lindroth Inc.; 84 br, Brown Brothers; 85, Historical Pictures Service, Chicago; 86, Culver Pictures; 87 tl, Bettmann Archive; 87 br, Brad Hamann; 89 tl, Robert P. Carr/Bruce Coleman Inc.; 89 inset, Michael O'Reilly/Joseph, Mindlin & Mulvey; 90–92 all, Tanya Rebelo/Joseph, Mindlin & Mulvey; 93, Bettmann Archive; 94, Dennis O'Brien/Joseph, Mindlin & Mulvey; 95 tl, John Rice/Joseph, Mindlin & Mulvey; 95 br, David Carlson/Evelyne Johnson Associates; 96 both, © Joe Viesti.

COVER CREDITS

Center; Western Publishing Company, Inc. Clockwise from top: H. Armstrong Roberts; Carl Roessler/Bruce Coleman Inc.; New York Convention and Visitors Bureau; Focus on Sports; Tom Powers/Joseph, Mindlin & Mulvey; Turi MacCombie/Evelyne Johnson Associates.

Library of Congress Catalog Card Number: 87-82741
ISBN: 0-307-70107-7

ABCDEFGHIJKLM

The letter *F* started with this symbol for the ancient Semitic word *waw*, meaning "hook."

The ancient Greeks used it along with another letter, *digamma*, that looked like our *F*.

When the ancient Romans borrowed it, they pronounced it and wrote it the way we do today.

F

fable

A fable is a story with a lesson. The characters are usually animals that talk and act like humans. The lesson is summed up in a *moral*—a wise saying that gives advice or tells something about human nature.

Fables have been told and retold for thousands of years. Most of the fables people tell

The fox who couldn't reach the grapes decided they must be sour anyway.

"There is comfort in pretending that what we can't get isn't worth having."

in Europe and the United States come from ancient Greece and India.

Aesop, who lived in Greece over 2,500 years ago, told many fables that we still know today. In one fable, a thirsty fox tries to pick a bunch of juicy grapes from a high branch. When he cannot reach them, he tells himself that they were probably sour anyway. Even today, when people find fault with things they cannot have, we call it "sour grapes."

Another popular fable told by Aesop is about a race between a tortoise and a hare. The tortoise is slow but steady. The hare is very fast, but so sure he will win that he does not pay attention to the race. In the end, the tortoise wins.

Fables are told in every part of the world. In India, there are hundreds of fables about animals. African fables first told in the United States by black slaves have become part of American literature.

See also **children's books.**

fairy

Fairies are imaginary creatures with magical powers. They are usually smaller than humans, but can change their size and shape, or even become invisible. Fairies can also fly, and do a great deal of work in an instant. Good fairies often use their powers to help humans. Wicked fairies cause trouble and may cast evil spells. For example, they may turn a prince into a frog. Elves, pixies, brownies, leprechauns, and gnomes are kinds of fairies.

A fairy rides on a dragonfly. Some fairies are pictured with wings of their own.

The tooth fairy is a favorite with American children. They believe she leaves money under their pillows in exchange for baby teeth that have fallen out.

People all over the world have stories about fairies. In some stories, fairies do all the housework. In others, a human might be a fairy's servant. There are stories about people who are rewarded for helping a fairy. Other stories tell of marriages between fairies and humans, or about fairy babies raised by human mothers.

Fairies were once feared. People believed they sometimes stole humans away, and made people lose their way. A person under a fairy's spell might fall asleep and not wake up for years. In a famous tale called "Sleeping Beauty," a fairy made a whole kingdom sleep for a hundred years!

See also **fairy tale.**

fairy tale

Fairy tales are stories about magic. They tell about wishes that come true, gifts that give the hero or heroine secret power, and magic creatures. They take place in a land that existed far away and long ago.

The hero or heroine of a fairy tale is often helped by fairies, elves, or a fairy godmother. Bad creatures—such as witches, giants, and ogres—try to keep the hero or heroine from reaching his or her goal. (*See* **fairy; giant;** and **witch.**)

Other characters found in fairy tales are stepmothers (usually wicked), kings and queens, princes and princesses, peasants, woodcutters, and fools. The fool in a fairy tale often turns out to be wise. Another common character in fairy tales is the talking animal. One of these is Puss-in-Boots, a cat who goes to the royal court and makes his owner rich and famous.

Magic tools help the hero or heroine. Aladdin's magic lamp was found in a pile of lost treasure. When Aladdin rubbed the lamp, a genie appeared who could make wishes come true. In "Cinderella," a fairy godmother gives Cinderella magic glass slippers. Characters in other stories find rings or coats that can make them invisible. Sometimes, a magic carpet or a pair of shoes helps the hero or heroine fly. Magic mirrors let a person see the future, the past, or what is happening in another part of the world.

Fairy tales almost always have happy endings. In fact, the most common last line of a fairy tale is ". . . and they lived happily ever after."

Famous Fairy Tales Many fairy tales are familiar to almost everyone. "Cinderella" is about a girl who is mistreated by her evil stepmother and stepsisters. Her fairy godmother turns Cinderella's ragged clothes into a beautiful gown and helps her go to a ball at the palace. There she meets the prince, who falls in love with her. "Little Red Riding Hood" is about a little girl who visits her grandmother and is almost eaten by a wolf. "Sleeping Beauty" is about a young woman who is put under a spell and sleeps for a hundred years. She wakes up when a young prince kisses her.

These three stories come from a famous collection of fairy tales, *Tales of Mother Goose,* gathered by Charles Perrault. The stories were put together in a book 300 years ago, but many were already hundreds of years old when the book first appeared.

Grimms' Fairy Tales is another famous collection. These stories were gathered by two German brothers, Jacob and Wilhelm Grimm. The Grimms heard the stories from old storytellers in German villages. These

"Rapunzel" (left) and "Little Red Riding Hood" (right) are popular fairy tales in which a young girl faces dangers and overcomes them.

storytellers themselves had heard the stories when they were young. No one knows when or where these tales were first told. The Grimm brothers published them about 150 years ago. (*See* **Grimm brothers.**)

Grimms' Fairy Tales includes the story "Hansel and Gretel," about a brother and sister who escape from a wicked witch in the forest. It also includes "Snow-White," about a beautiful girl who is almost murdered by her jealous stepmother. She is rescued by seven dwarfs.

Most fairy tales are so old that no one knows who first told them. Some, however, were written by people we know about. Hans Christian Andersen wrote many fairy tales in the 1800s. "The Little Mermaid" is about a mermaid who falls in love with a human being. "The Ugly Duckling" is about a baby bird who hatches in the nest of a duck. The mother duck and all the ducklings make fun of the ugly duckling. But the ugly duckling grows up to be a beautiful swan. (*See* **Andersen, Hans Christian.**)

The oldest fairy tale we know comes from a book written in China more than 1,000 years ago. It tells of a girl who has a fish for a friend. Her stepmother kills the fish, but the girl learns that the fish's bones will make her wishes come true. She wishes for a dress and gold shoes to wear to a festival. There, she loses one of the shoes. Someone sells the shoe to the king. The king searches everywhere for the shoe's owner. When he finds the girl, he marries her.

This Chinese story probably reminds you of Cinderella and her glass slipper. Some people think all the old fairy tales were created at the same time and place, thousands of years ago in India. It is very likely, however, that similar stories were invented by different people in many parts of the world.

Today, fairy tales are mainly for children. Long ago, adults liked to listen to such stories, too. For them, it was a way of learning about the world. Most people couldn't read, so they needed to hear stories that could be remembered. Fairy tales about wonderful events and magical characters were interesting and easy to remember.

See also **children's books.**

---

fall, *see* **season**

The nuclear family includes parents and children (left).
Many families are made up of one parent and one or more children.

family

You are part of a family. So is everyone else in the world. Families are very important to human beings. For this reason, families probably have existed as long as humans have lived on the earth.

A new family is formed when a man and woman agree to share their lives. This small family grows when the couple have or adopt children. A family may also include foster children—children who are not adopted but live with people who are not their parents. Usually, the members of a family unit live together in one household.

Why Families Are Necessary Families help their members in many ways. One of the most important ways is to provide warmth, love, and security. People need the closeness that a family offers.

Another reason families exist is to raise children. Families don't just bring children into the world. They also take care of them until the children grow up and can take care of themselves. The family teaches children their language, their religion, and the customs of their society. It teaches them health and safety habits to guide them for the rest of their lives. It also teaches them values

such as honesty and respect for others. Perhaps most important, the family teaches self-reliance. If it did not, young people would never be ready to go off and start new families of their own.

Besides caring for its children, a family also looks after family members who are sick, poor, or aged.

Different Kinds of Families People all over the world belong to families of some kind. Some kinds of families may seem strange to us. What seems normal to us, however, may seem odd to others.

For example, we often think of a family as a mother, a father, and their children living together under one roof. This kind of family, called the *nuclear family,* is very common. But other kinds of families are almost equally common. One is called the *single-parent family*—one parent and her or his children. There may be just one parent because divorce or death has split up a husband and wife. Or it may be that the mother and father never agreed to share their lives permanently.

Another kind of family is called the *extended family.* It consists of more than two generations living together. There may be grandparents, parents, and children. When a

In an extended family, children, parents, and grandparents live in one house. If extended families do not live together, they may get together for celebrations.

woman in India gets married, she usually goes to live with her husband in his parents' home. If the parents have many sons, this family can grow to be quite large.

In another kind of extended family, a man has more than one wife at the same time. Some peoples in Africa follow this custom, called *polygamy.* In other places, a woman may have more than one husband at the same time. This practice is called *polyandry.*

Some different family patterns involve special ways of bringing up children. In Sparta, a city of ancient Greece, the people were very warlike. Young boys left home at the age of seven and moved in with other youths to begin a long period of army training.

In some settlements in Israel, children never live with their parents. Instead, they live nearby with other children their own age in separate houses for children. They visit their parents on weekends.

In Samoa, which is an island group in the Pacific Ocean, children may or may not live with their parents. They often stay for a few months at a time with different relatives. Then they move in with the family they like best.

Changes in the U.S. Family In the early days of the United States, most people were farmers. Everybody in the family, except for very young children, had farm chores to do. The family not only lived together but worked together.

This situation changed in the late 1800s. More and more people left their farms and moved to cities. Men got jobs in offices and factories to support their families. Their wives stayed home to take care of the children and run the household. In most families, the husband was the "breadwinner." This meant that he earned the money to buy bread—and everything else. The woman was the "homemaker." Her job was to turn an ordinary house into a cozy home.

Now the family has changed further. It is no longer so common for a married woman to be a homemaker. In fact, over half of all married women in the United States work outside the home. Women want careers. Families need the extra money, too.

In earlier days, there were strict divisions between "men's work" and "women's work." Women hardly ever became doctors or lawyers or went into politics. Men rarely took care of children or cooked a meal. Today, few people are surprised to see a woman doctor treating patients, or a father taking care of the children.

If parents work, children may spend workdays in a day-care center.

These changes in the kinds of work husbands and wives do have brought other changes in the family. In the past, the man of the house ruled the family like a king. His wife could not vote or own property, and she had little voice in family decisions. Today, there is greater equality in families. Women now vote and own property. The husband and the wife make many family decisions together.

With mothers and fathers both working outside the home, many families can no longer take care of grandparents or other older family members. Many old people now live in special apartments or homes for the aged. Working parents also need help if they have young children. Many small children play and learn with others in day-care centers.

Family Problems One of the most serious problems facing families is *divorce*—the end of a marriage.

Single-parent families have problems of their own. Many of them are poor. This is mainly because most single-parent families are headed by women, and women often make less money than men do. In any case, being a single parent and a working parent is hard. There is no one to share the many responsibilities.

Another cause of family problems is illness, especially if it lasts for a long time. All family members feel the strain if a parent drinks too much or if any family member is seriously ill or handicapped.

Specially trained family counselors can help families in trouble. Counselors can meet with family members and help them handle their problems.

All families have their ups and downs. Love, understanding, respect, and cooperation help families deal with problems and still enjoy being a family.

See also **adoption; divorce;** and **marriage.**

Faraday, Michael

Michael Faraday lived in England from 1791 to 1867. His discoveries made possible many of the modern electrical conveniences that we enjoy today.

Times were hard in London when Faraday was young. His family could not afford to send him to school. Instead, he went to work at a shop where books were bound and sold. He took every opportunity to learn from the books around him. With the money he earned, he bought materials for experiments. In 1813, he became the assistant to a famous scientist of the time, Sir Humphry Davy.

Faraday soon began experimenting on his own with chemistry and electricity. His most useful discovery was the electric generator.

Faraday's generator made electricity when he turned the crank.

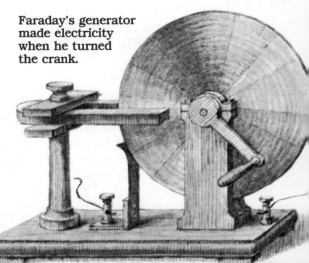

He also built the first electric motors. His ideas later helped James Clerk Maxwell explain electromagnetism.

Faraday earned degrees and awards from many universities. He was also offered many business opportunities. But he preferred living a simple life in a home provided for him by the queen of England.

See also **generator** and **electricity.**

farm animal

"Old McDonald had a farm." In the nursery song, McDonald's farm was filled with the sounds of farm animals—some of the many animals raised for food and clothing.

Animals that people keep on a farm are kinds that people have tamed. The animals are used to living with people, and they rely on people for their food and shelter. People take good care of the animals they raise because the animals provide many kinds of food—especially milk, eggs, and meat. Some animals also have coats of fur that can be made into clothing. Sheep's coats—*fleeces* —are made into wool for blankets, sweaters, and other clothes.

Different animals are raised on different kinds of farms. Beef cattle are *range animals.* They are often raised on large ranches. Cattle are very hardy, and can travel many miles looking for grasses and other small plants to eat. Beef cattle spend most of their lives on the range. But a few weeks or months before they are to be butchered, they are brought to a feedlot. There they are fed grains to help them gain weight.

Beef cattle provide us with many different cuts of beef, including steaks, stewing meats, and ground beef for hamburgers. (*See* **beef** and **cattle.**)

Dairy cattle are another important group of farm animals. They cannot travel as far as beef cattle, and they need richer grass to eat. On a dairy farm, the female cattle— cows—graze in pastures all day. At night, they come home to a barn to be milked. Dairy cows must be milked two or even three times a day. If the farmer stops milking them, they stop giving milk.

People have kept animals for their milk for thousands of years. In other parts of the world, people use the milk of sheep, goats, horses, water buffalo, and camels.

These hogs are being raised on a family farm in Iowa. They eat corn grown on the farm. Hogs provide pork chops, bacon, ham, and other cuts of fresh and preserved meat.

farm animal

Pigs—also called *swine* or *hogs*—are important farm animals. Many pigs are raised in the midwestern United States. First, they grow big and fat. Then, they are butchered for their meat. Bacon, ham, spare ribs, and pork chops are some of the most popular meats we get from pigs.

Farm birds—chickens, ducks, turkeys, and geese—are known as *poultry*. Until recently, poultry grew up outdoors in farmyards, near the barn and farmhouse. Today, most poultry are raised on special indoor farms where every part of their lives is controlled. At a poultry farm, a chicken or turkey spends its whole life in a single small wire cage. It receives its food on a belt that passes through the cage. The temperature and light in the cages is controlled and steady.

Frying and roasting chickens are raised this way. They are usually sold for market about eight weeks after hatching. Chickens bred to lay eggs are raised in similar places. They never leave their cages, and the eggs roll away to be gathered by machines. (*See* **poultry**.)

In earlier times, some farm animals were kept to do hard work. Farmers kept oxen or horses to pull plows and pull wagonloads of crops to market. Today, this work is done by machine, but farmers may still keep horses for riding or as pets.

See also **farming** and **dairying**.

**These chickens are being raised for their meat.
Other chickens, called *layers,* are raised for the eggs they lay.**

These farms grow field crops, using machinery to plant, cultivate, and harvest. Still, the farmer at bottom keeps a garden for his own family.

farming

Farming—often called *agriculture*—is the business of growing crops or raising animals for use by people. Even though you may not live near a farm, farming is really part of your everyday life.

Just think of what you eat each day and where it comes from. Imagine that you have just eaten a chicken salad and lettuce sandwich on wheat bread with a glass of milk and an orange. The chicken may have come from a poultry farm in Maryland, and the lettuce from a farm in California. The wheat may have come from a huge farm in Nebraska, the milk from a dairy farm in Wisconsin, and the orange from a citrus grove in Florida. Each part of your meal got to your table from a different part of the country or even a different part of the world. Over nine-tenths of the world's food is grown on farms.

A Farmer's Choices A farmer must first decide which crops to grow or which animals to raise. The farmer has to consider what will work best on a particular piece of land at a given time.

First, there are the growing conditions. Some crops, such as citrus fruits, need a long, mild growing season. Other crops, such as grains, can handle a harsh winter. Some crops, such as apples, can be grown only where it is cold in the winter and mild in the summer.

Other important growing conditions include the amount of water and the kind of soil. The sandy soil and warm climate of Florida is good for growing citrus fruits such as oranges and lemons. But the fertile fields and temperate climate of Iowa are better suited to corn and soybeans.

Which foods people want and how easily the farmer can get the foods to market are other things to consider. Some fruits must

11

Picking vegetable and fruit crops is hard work. These migrant workers are picking tomatoes in a field in Florida.

be harvested quickly and sold within days, or they will spoil. Others can be picked green and will ripen on the way to market.

Farming in the United States The farms of the United States produce a tremendous amount of food. Just two-thirds of the grain grown in the vast fields of the nation's heartland is enough to supply the country with bread. The remaining one-third of this grain is sold and sent to other nations. Food is an important export of the United States.

Every year, farmers in the United States grow crops on over 350 million acres of land. Because of the different weather and soil conditions, a great variety of fruits and vegetables are grown—from apples to zucchini.

Most of the farms in the United States started as family farms. The land was handed down from generation to generation. The family lived on the land. They grew enough food to feed themselves. In addition, they produced one or more "cash crops"—products that they sold.

Family farmers must be good managers to grow food and get it to market. They must buy machinery to plow the land and harvest their crops. They must buy fertilizers to improve the soil, and food for their farm animals. Farm families work together and often

hire workers to plant and harvest. After the harvest, farmers sell the food. They sell grains to grain companies. They sell milk to dairies that package and sell milk products to stores. Farm animals, such as cattle and pigs, are sold to meat processors.

Today, there are fewer family farms. Many American farms are very large and often are run as big businesses. Large corporations own farms. They hire people to work on these farms.

Today's farms are very specialized. There are poultry farms for chickens, dairy farms for milk, and farms just for grains. A specialized farm uses special machinery for the crop or animal it raises.

Farms now need fewer workers, because of big machines and other improvements. In 1800, most of the people in the United States were farmers. Today, only one American in 14 works on a farm.

Farming Around the World Some other countries—such as Canada, Japan, and the Soviet Union—have many large farms using modern machinery.

In many tropical countries, however, some people still grow just enough food for their families. Very often, over half of the crops grown in a village are used by the people there and are not sold elsewhere. In many cases, the people lack machinery. They must do the hard farm work by hand, using methods that are ages old. Today, many people in tropical countries live in cities. They no longer grow their own food. These nations must import food or their people will starve.

In parts of Africa, Asia, and South America, much land is owned by a few wealthy people. Many poor farmers in these regions have little land on which to grow food. Water shortages may prevent farmers from irrigating their crops. As the population increases in nations that cannot grow enough food, so does the threat of starvation.

The Future of Farming Growing enough food for all the world's people is everyone's problem. Scientists are looking for new ways to keep soil rich and bring water to dry lands. They work with farmers to keep good soil from being washed away. They also look for better ways to protect water from pollution, and to cut down on the amount of water that is wasted.

Scientists have also begun to breed "super-plants" and "super-animals." These are kinds that grow quickly, resist disease, and can grow under many different conditions.

These terraced fields in Asia hold in water to grow rice.

It is important that improved ways of farming be shared around the world. Only if nations work together can the problems of the world's food supply be solved.

See also **dairying; farm animal;** and **farm machinery.**

farm machinery

If you have ever seen a tractor in a field or on the road, you have seen one of the most common farm machines. Farmers use all kinds of machinery to make the job of growing crops or raising animals easier. That is why just one U.S. farm worker can provide enough food for about 40 people.

Plowing the Soil Before crops are planted, the soil must be prepared. Since ancient times, people have used wooden or metal devices called *plows* to dig trenches, or *furrows*, in which seeds could be planted. Often, animals were used to pull the plows. Today, farmers use tractors to drag a plow across the field. The plow is like a knife that cuts into the soil. But the knife is curved, so the soil turns over after it is cut.

The soil is still in large clumps after plowing. To break it up for planting, farmers use a *disc harrow.* This machine has a row of metal discs with sharp edges. As the tractor moves, the discs turn and break up the clumps.

Another kind of harrow has many metal teeth, like a rake. It follows behind a tractor and breaks up any lumps of earth that remain after discing.

Planting Crops Special machines help farmers plant their crops. *Planters* are farm machines used for planting crops that grow in rows. Corn, soybeans, cotton, potatoes, and tobacco are all row crops. These machines carry seeds and also some fertilizer to help the young seedlings grow. The kind of planter used depends on how big the seeds are. The planter can sow the seeds and add fertilizer to several plowed rows at once.

Hay, rice, wheat, and some other crops are not grown in rows. The seeds for these plants are just scattered—*broadcast*—over the field. A *broadcaster* is used for planting some of these crops. It has a wide-mouthed tube that shoots seeds over the ground.

Grains, such as wheat, are sometimes planted with a *drill.* A drill is a metal tube that pokes a hole in the ground, drops fertilizer and seeds into the hole, and then covers it up.

Once the seeds are planted, the farmer's work is far from over. The young plants must be *cultivated*—kept free from weeds. A machine called a *cultivator* does this job. It is like several small plows that are pulled together. Each of the cultivator blades turns over about an inch (2.5 centimeters) of soil, to kill weeds.

Fertilizer may be fed to the growing plants with a machine called a *spreader.* Often, insecticides in a liquid form are sprayed on the crops to kill insects that would otherwise damage the plants.

Harvesting Machines When a crop is ready for picking, it is harvesttime. The most important piece of equipment, and often the most expensive, is the *combine.* The name means "combined harvester and thresher." Combining two jobs into one makes the harvesting work easier and faster.

Above, a *harrow*—a kind of light plow. Below, a plow that was pulled by a horse.

This corn harvester pulls a corn ear from the plant, takes the husk off the ear, and separates the kernels from the corncob. It spits the kernels into the truck at right.

This planter is digging holes and planting soybeans automatically.

A combine has a sharp edge for cutting off the tops of grain plants, such as wheat. Then it separates the grains from the stalk.

Many crops require special harvesting machines. For corn, there are *corn pickers and huskers.* For cotton, there are *cotton strippers.* They take cotton bolls off the plant and separate the fluffy cotton from its hard covering. Root vegetables, such as potatoes, need special pickers that reach under the ground to harvest the crop. To make bales of hay, mowers first cut down grass. After it dries, *balers* compress it, form it into even piles, and wrap wire around it.

Many of these farm machines are attachments that farmers can hitch onto a tractor. Large tractors have an air-conditioned cab for the driver. They usually have automatic gears and are even equipped with computers. They help farmers control the speed of planting and harvesting.

Dairy and Poultry Farm Machines Dairy farmers raise cows for their milk. Many use *milking machines* to milk their cows two or three times a day. The machines can also measure how much milk the cows give each time and keep track of the amount.

On poultry farms, chickens and turkeys are fed by a machine that pours out just the right amount of food each time. Other machines collect the eggs. Almost all the jobs around a poultry farm can be done by machines. This means that thousands of animals can be raised by a very small number of people.

See also **dairying** and **farming.**

On the Great Plains of eastern Colorado, giant wheat harvesters use headlights as they begin their work before sunrise. They can harvest night and day.

fashion

Europe 1750s

Greece 300s B.C.

North America 1870s

People like to dress in the same fashion as others of their age and country.
Using a particular fashion well can also make a person attractive to others.

fashion

Fashions are the styles people prefer during certain periods of time. We may speak of the "latest fashion" in hairstyles, cars, furniture or toys. Most often, when we say "fashion," we mean clothing.

Styles go out of fashion and come back into fashion. For example, in the 1770s, fashionable women wore hairstyles 3 feet (1 meter) high! American pioneer men like Daniel Boone wore their hair in long ponytails and dressed much like Indians. In the 1960s, men's hair reached the collar, then the shoulders again. Women wore their hair long, and sometimes piled it on top of their heads. Recently, men and women have worn their hair short, but the fashion keeps changing every few years.

Women's skirt lengths is another fashion that changes often. Sometimes, the popular style calls for skirts above the knee. The miniskirts of the 1960s made long dresses look "old-fashioned." When longer skirts became stylish again, miniskirts looked old-fashioned.

There are many reasons why fashions change. New inventions, such as zippers, changed the look of clothing. So did modern synthetic fabrics. Chemical waving lotions and wire rollers changed women's hairstyles. Styles from different parts of the world influence fashion. A country's laws may cause changes. Changes in the way people live may bring changes in clothing fashions. The ideas of one person may bring changes.

Paintings of history's famous people show how fashions have changed. For example, the first five presidents of the United States did not wear long trousers. They wore knee-length *breeches* and long stockings. John Quincy Adams was the first president to wear long trousers. Trousers were a new fashion from England.

One person who helped change fashion was Amelia Bloomer. In the late 1800s, women wore tight corsets and long skirts. She thought women should wear comfortable clothing. She suggested loose pants under a short dress. These new pants were called *bloomers,* after Amelia Bloomer.

16

North America 1960s

Many fashion changes took place when Europeans began trading for foreign goods. Bright silk fabrics reached Europe in the 1300s. Wealthy people dressed in the rich new fabric. Some countries made laws about who could wear expensive fabrics. After America was discovered, furs from North America reached Europe. Soon, wealthy Europeans were wearing beaver hats, fur collars, and fur coats. Most poor people could not buy silk, velvet, or fur. They wore the same plain clothes every day.

Most changes in fashion seem to happen by themselves. Often, no one can explain why people suddenly like a certain fashion, and then just as suddenly drop it and take up another.

Sometimes, changes are forced on people. Peter the Great ruled Russia from 1682 to 1725. He wanted Russians to dress like people in other parts of Europe. He forced Russian men to shave off their beards, wear pants instead of robes, and stop wearing cone-shaped hats.

In Turkey in the 1930s, Kemal Ataturk, too, tried to "westernize" his country. He outlawed the fez, a red hat worn by men, and the veil that covered a woman's face and body. In the late 1970s, Islamic leaders came to rule Iran. Iranian women had to stop wearing European clothing and instead follow Islamic rules for dress. One of these rules is that women must wear a long veil.

Changes in how people live have brought many changes in fashion. As people began to enjoy exercising and sports, they wanted clothing that was easier to move in and to clean. Blue jeans, which were once only work clothes for men, became popular for everyday wear. Boys began wearing jeans to school. Then girls, too, began wearing jeans or other slacks to school. As fashions changed, school rules changed, too.

Today, many people earn their living by designing new fabrics, clothing styles, makeup, shoes, hairdos, perfumes, and jewelry. Each season, clothing stores sell the new styles.

You will see many fashions change during your life. Some fashions change so slowly you hardly notice. Others happen suddenly, and everybody talks about them.

See also **clothing; jewelry; hat; shoes; toy; furniture;** and **architecture.**

Hairstyles, like styles in clothing, change often.

powdered wig

beehive

spikes

cornrows

spit curls

fat

Fat is one of the six kinds of essential foods. It is found in both plants and animals. Lard is a kind of animal fat left over when meat has been cooked. Butter is an animal fat made from milk. Lard and butter are solids at room temperature. Two plant fats are corn oil and peanut oil. They are liquids at room temperature. Fats are found in many different kinds of food, such as milk, fish, and nuts.

You can do a test to see if a food has very much fat in it. Rub some of the food on a piece of brown paper. Let the paper dry. Then hold the paper up to the light. If there is a spot that lets the light come through, the food has a lot of fat in it.

Your own body makes fat. When you eat foods that contain more energy than you need, your body stores some of the extra energy as fat. A small amount of fat in your body is good for you. Fat around some of your body organs acts as a cushion against

Fats come from meats, nuts, and milk products, and from oils in which foods are fried.

injury. A larger layer of fat just under your skin helps you stay warm in cold weather.

It is not hard for most people to get enough fat in their diets. Many fast foods such as hamburgers and french-fried potatoes have lots of fat. Snack foods such as potato chips and cookies are also rich in fat. In fact, most people need to be careful not to eat too much fat. A diet high in fat can provide more energy than the body needs. This extra energy can make the body build up too much fat.

Eating too much fat may cause other health problems as well. Fats in the diet can cause a waxy substance to build up on the walls of the blood vessels. Blood may be blocked from reaching important organs like the heart and brain. This can cause heart attacks and strokes. (*See* **heart disease.**)

Fats are used in manufacturing many products. Soap, paint, cosmetics, and candles are just a few of them.

See also **nutrition.**

Fathers of Confederation

The Fathers of Confederation were a group of 33 Canadian patriots who helped make Canada the democratic nation that it is today. As a result of their meetings in the 1860s, the different parts of Canada were united under one national government.

Canada was known as British North America in the mid-1800s. Upper Canada (now Ontario) had many British settlers. Most of the people of Lower Canada (now Quebec) were descended from French settlers. Upper and Lower Canada together were known as the Province of Canada. Along the Atlantic coast lay the Maritime Provinces of Nova Scotia, New Brunswick, and Prince Edward Island. To the west of Upper Canada were vast unsettled prairies and plains. British Columbia was on the Pacific coast.

British North America had its share of problems. Transportation across such a huge land was difficult. The leaders of the

The men pictured above met in 1864 to prepare for Canada's self-government. They arranged for separate territories (right) to form a confederation—a single nation.

government worried that the mostly unsettled area between the east and west coasts would be claimed by people moving north from the United States.

Great Britain had allowed the colonists in British North America to make their own laws. But there were problems with this in the Province of Canada, because the British and French Canadians could not get along. Sharp differences existed between the two major political parties, and neither one could gain control. In 1864, George Brown of the Liberal party and John A. Macdonald and George Étienne Cartier of the Conservative party agreed to work together. They hoped to unify all of British North America.

In September 1864, eight leaders, including Macdonald, Brown, and Cartier, traveled to Charlottetown, Prince Edward Island. Leaders of the Maritime Provinces were meeting there to discuss forming their own union. The two groups agreed to meet in Quebec to discuss the creation of one national government.

The Quebec Conference of 1864 was attended by 33 representatives from all the provinces. At the conference, a plan for creating a union was written. Within a few years, most of the provinces approved the plan. In 1867, the British North America Act was passed and the Dominion of Canada was created. The dominion united Ontario, Quebec, Nova Scotia, and New Brunswick. Over the years, ten other provinces and two territories joined the union. Today, a united Canada stretches from the Atlantic to the Pacific coasts.

See also **Canada** and **Macdonald, John A.**

19

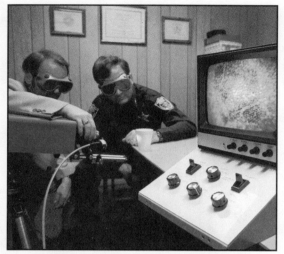

An FBI agent (left) uses a laser to "read" a fingerprint on a plastic cup.

Federal Bureau of Investigation

The Federal Bureau of Investigation (FBI) is one of the best-known agencies of the U. S. government. About 20,000 people work for the FBI. Its headquarters are in Washington, D.C. It has offices in all the states, Puerto Rico, and 15 foreign countries.

The laws of the U.S. say that certain crimes will be handled by cities, and certain other crimes will be handled by states. The rest will be the responsibility of the U.S. government. These are called *federal crimes*. One of the most important tasks of the FBI is to investigate federal crimes. The people who do the investigating are called *special agents*. They make up about a third of all FBI employees.

Special agents collect information on such serious crimes as kidnappings, bombings, hijackings, and bank robberies. They may investigate other robberies, too, if more than one state is involved. They fight against organized crime—groups that make a living from illegal activities such as drug dealing. Special agents also try to learn about people who might be dangerous to the security of the United States, such as terrorists. Another important part of the FBI's job is to keep people from spying on the United States and from selling secret information to other countries.

To be a special agent, a person must be a U.S. citizen between the ages of 23 and 34. Agents usually have college degrees in law or accounting. The FBI also hires engineers, scientists, and people who can speak more than one language. Special agents attend a 15-week training program at the FBI National Academy in Quantico, Virginia.

Besides investigating crimes, the FBI helps the police of states, counties, and cities solve crimes. To do this, the FBI has one of the world's best crime laboratories. Its experts examine over 600,000 pieces of evidence every year, from firearms and bullets to handwriting. They can learn a great deal from tiny bits of cloth and hair found at the scene of a crime. They can also identify automobiles using paint samples.

The FBI has the world's largest collection of fingerprints—over 175 million sets. The FBI also helps police through its National Crime Information Center. This center has information stored in computers about 5 million crime cases and suspected criminals. This system handles more than 170,000 requests for information every day.

See also **crime** and **fingerprint.**

fern

Ferns look like feathery leaves growing straight out of the ground. Usually, each leaf is divided into smaller leaflets. Most fern leaves are tightly curled up when they begin to grow. These curled leaves are called *fiddleheads,* because they are shaped like the head of a fiddle. The fiddleheads open into full-size leaves.

You will often find ferns growing on the floor of a forest. Here the ferns get the shade and moisture they need. Ferns rarely grow in sunny, open areas.

Ferns grow all over the world, in both hot and cold climates. Most are found in warm, tropical places. Ferns are usually less than 1 meter (3¼ feet) tall. But some ferns as big as trees grow in tropical places. Tree ferns may grow as tall as 15 meters (50 feet).

It is easy to tell ferns from flowering plants. Ferns reproduce in two stages, starting with tiny structures called *spores*. If you look at the underside of a fern leaf, you will see colored spots. These spots, the *spore cases*, are usually brown. They are where the spores form. A single fern leaf may produce more than a million spores.

When the spores are ripe, the spore cases break open. The spores are so small that they look like dust. If a spore falls onto moist soil, it will sprout. A small, heart-shaped plant grows from the spore. This plant is only about half a centimeter (¼ inch) across. You can find the small plants if you look carefully.

In the second stage, the heart-shaped plant produces eggs and sperm. An egg and a sperm join to form a single cell. The full-size fern grows from that cell.

People have used ferns in many ways. Once, fern leaves were used to make soft beds. In some tropical areas, fern leaves are used to make roofs on houses. Ferns have an underground stem called a *rhizome*. American Indians cooked and ate the rhizomes of sword ferns and lady ferns. People also eat some fiddleheads. The leaves of the licorice

climbing fern

maidenhead fern

fern have been used in place of sugar and as a flavoring.

In the past, some ferns were used as medicines. The goldenback fern was used to treat toothaches. The bird's-foot fern was used for nosebleeds. The licorice fern was used for sore throats. One of the most common ways we use ferns today is as houseplants and in gardens.

See also **plant.**

A single fern frond usually has many leaflets branching off two by two. The maidenhair fern (above) is a favorite houseplant.

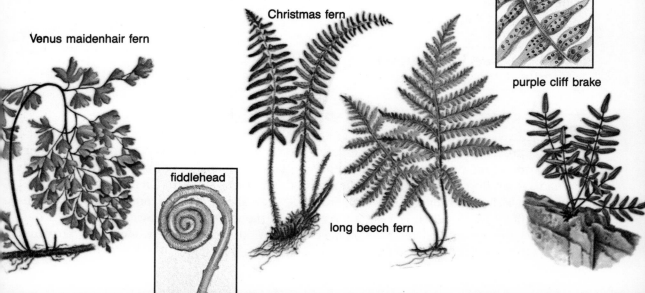

Venus maidenhair fern

Christmas fern

fiddlehead

long beech fern

spores

purple cliff brake

Fertile Crescent, *see* Babylonia; Sumer

fertilizer

Fertilizer is anything people add to soil to help plants grow. Plants can use energy from the sun to make their own food. But they also need minerals from the soil. Fertilizer can provide some of these minerals.

Since ancient times, people have used animal manure and other natural materials to help plants grow. Today, millions of tons of fertilizers are used by farmers around the world.

The most important elements that plants get from fertilizers are nitrogen, phosphorus, and potassium. Many fertilizers contain all of these elements. A bag of fertilizer may be marked 5-10-10. This means it has 5 percent nitrogen, 10 percent phosphorus compound, and 10 percent potassium compound. Most fertilizers also have small amounts of other elements.

Fertilizers made from materials found in nature, such as animal manure or powdered animal bones, are called *organic fertilizers.* Fertilizers manufactured from such chemicals as ammonia are called *synthetic fertilizers.* Both kinds must be used and stored properly. Too much fertilizer can harm the plants and their environment.

See also **plant** and **farming.**

feudalism, *see* knighthood; Middle Ages

fever

You have probably had someone take your temperature when you were sick, to see if you had a fever. Fever is a rise in the temperature of the body. The average body temperature is 98.6° F (37° C). When you get a fever, your body temperature may reach as high as 105° F (41° C).

Fevers have many different causes. Some doctors believe that the body raises its temperature in order to kill the organisms that are causing an infection. So in some cases, a fever may help the body get well. Many diseases—such as flu, measles, and mumps—can cause fevers.

A fever may last for several days. During that time, the fever goes through stages. At first, you feel weak and cold. You do not feel like eating. Soon your skin feels hot and dry. You sleep poorly and have strange dreams. During the last stage, the fever breaks. Your temperature falls. Your skin gets moist. Then you begin to feel better.

A cold cloth on the forehead may help make a person with a fever more comfortable. When a fever is high, doctors sometimes suggest bathing the person in cool water to lower body temperature. Medicines such as aspirin can be given to reduce fevers. But aspirin should *not* be used to lower a child's or teenager's fever unless a doctor recommends it.

See also **disease and sickness.**

Fokker

S.P.A.D.

fighter plane

A fighter plane is an airplane designed to attack and destroy enemy airplanes. Fighter planes were made before World War I. One of the first was made in Great Britain in 1913. It was called *Destroyer,* and it had a machine gun mounted in the nose. An engine in the back pushed the two-winged airplane through the air.

Northrop P.61
Black Widow

Spitfire

JU-87
Stuka

Fighter planes were first used in World
War I (left). Many special fighters
were built for World War II (above).
The Black Widow was a U.S. night fighter.
The Spitfire was a British fighter.
The Stuka was a German dive bomber.

Fighter Planes of World War I Fighter
planes were first used in World War I, from
1914 through 1918. At the beginning of the
war, "spotter" airplanes would fly over the
enemy armies to keep track of where the soldiers were. These airplanes did not have
guns, but pilots carried pistols and rifles.

The first fighter planes were just spotter
planes with machine guns on them. Most of
the time the machine guns were in front of
the pilot. There were no jet engines then, so
most planes also had a propeller in front of
the pilot. Shots often hit the propeller. In
1915, a device called a *synchronizer* was invented. It made the bullets go between the
propeller blades without hitting them. These
airplanes were used to shoot down balloons
and other airplanes. When two fighter
planes attacked each other, it was called a
"dogfight." Fighter planes would also shoot
at targets on the ground.

Some World War I fighter planes had cannons. Some even had small rockets attached
to the wings. But the cannons and rockets
were not as accurate as machine guns.

Early fighter planes had a wood frame covered with cloth. Most of them could fly only
about 70 or 80 miles (113 to 129 kilometers)
per hour. That was very fast back then!

Toward the end of the war, faster planes
were made. The German Fokker and the
French Spad could fly 135 miles (217 kilometers) per hour. (*See* **World War I.**)

Planes of World War II By the time
World War II began, in 1939, fighter planes
had improved. The fighter planes used in
World War II were usually made completely
of metal. They were much stronger than the
ones made of wood and cloth. Some carried
cannons in addition to machine guns. These
fighter planes could fly much faster, too.

The British Spitfire, for example, could fly
over 350 miles (563 kilometers) per hour. It
had eight machine guns. Some others could
fly 450 miles (725 kilometers) per hour.
Among the famous fighter planes used in

World War II were the German Messer-schmitt, the British Hurricane and Spitfire, the Japanese Zero, and the American P-47 Thunderbolt and P-51 Mustang.

Fighter planes in World War II were used to shoot down enemy airplanes and to escort larger planes, called *bombers* to their targets. If enemy airplanes attacked the bombers, the fighters went after the enemy planes.

During World War II, many fighter planes took off and landed on *aircraft carriers* —huge ships with flat decks. This meant that fighter planes could be used where there were no landing fields. Many air battles in World War II were fought by fighter planes from aircraft carriers far from land. (*See* **World War II.**)

Modern Fighter Planes Most of the fighter planes used after World War II were jet-powered. The American Sabre and the Soviet MiG were the two most famous fighter planes of the Korean War in the early 1950s. These jet planes could fly much faster and higher than propeller airplanes.

Since the 1950s, all new fighter planes have been jets. Today, a fighter jet can fly faster than 1,000 miles per hour (1,600 kilometers per hour). This is much faster than the speed of sound. The planes are called *supersonic,* which means "faster than sound."

Today's fighter planes have radar and computers that help them fly in all kinds of weather. They also use their radar and computers to find and destroy enemy airplanes.

Modern fighter planes carry many kinds of weapons. Some carry machine guns and cannons. Many carry *air-to-air missiles* that can shoot down other planes. Some use bombs and *air-to-surface missiles* to attack targets on the ground. Fighter planes that carry bombs are called *fighter-bombers.*

Many modern fighters can take off from the ground or from aircraft carriers. Some can even take off and land straight up and down, like helicopters. Ever since they were first used, fighter planes have been important weapons in every war.

See also **aircraft.**

The F-16 is a modern jet fighter plane. The jet intake is just under the cockpit. Air-to-air rockets can be strapped underneath the plane's fuselage (left).

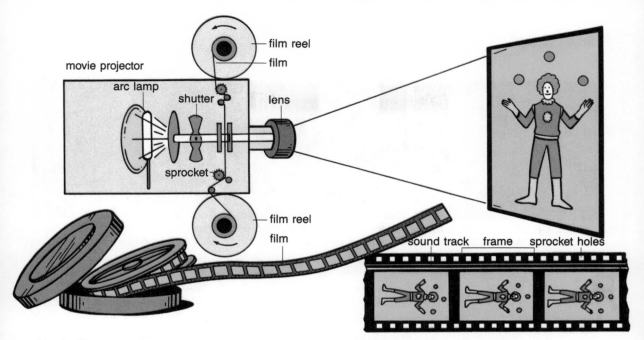

Movie film runs through a projector (top). The film (bottom) is made of hundreds of small still pictures. The sound track is along the side of the film.

Fiji, *see* Pacific Islands

Fillmore, Millard, *see* presidents of the U.S.

filmmaking

Have you ever wondered how a movie camera works? Have you ever wanted to know how a movie projector makes a picture seem to move? This entry tells how these two machines are used to make motion pictures. It also tells about some of the people whose special skills make motion pictures so lifelike and exciting. You can read more about motion pictures at the entry **movie.**

Moving pictures—also called *films* or just *movies*—were invented about 100 years ago. Videotape was invented in the 1950s. Today, people use film and videotape to record family and community events. People in filmmaking and video clubs share equipment and work together. You may have used video or film in school projects.

Making Pictures Move When you use an ordinary camera to take "snapshots" of your friends, the camera takes one picture every time you snap the shutter. But when you

use a movie camera, the camera takes many pictures each second. When you show a movie, the *projector* shows many pictures each second. On the screen, you see the pictures so quickly that they look like one picture in which things are moving!

One way to learn how filmmaking works is to study a strip of movie film. Each small picture is called a *frame.* If you look closely, you can see that each picture is a little different from the one before it.

Along the edges of the film are small holes called *sprocket holes.* The movie projector has sets of small wheels with *sprockets* —tiny pins or teeth. As the wheels turn, the sprockets fit into the holes and move the film past the projector's lens and lamp. The sprocket wheels move the film at a rate of 24 frames per second.

A 10-second scene of a car speeding toward you is made up of 240 separate frames. If you look at the frames one after the other, it is difficult to see how they are different. The car in the second frame looks very much the way it does in the first. But if you compare the last frame with the first, you can see how much the picture has changed. In the first frame, the car is tiny and looks far away. By the 240th frame, the car is the largest thing in the frame and looks very close.

In single-frame filming, a movie camera takes one picture each hour. When the film is shown at normal speed, a flower seems to bloom in seconds rather than days.

Film can be black-and-white or color. It is *unexposed* when you buy it. When you "shoot" a movie with the camera, light reaches the film and causes chemical changes in it. After film has been shot, we say that it has been *exposed*. Before you can see results, exposed film needs to be *developed* in a film laboratory. After that, it can be shown on a film projector.

Slow Motion and Fast Motion Most movie projectors show only 24 frames per second. In order to show slow motion, the camera must first shoot more than 24 frames per second.

For example, if a two-second motorcycle jump is filmed at normal speed, 48 frames are taken. If the same jump is filmed with the camera taking 120 frames per second, the motorcycle jump appears on 240 frames. When the film is projected at 24 frames per second, the two-second jump lasts for ten seconds.

There are slow-motion cameras that can take more than 1,000 frames per second. Super-slow motion can let us see how a hummingbird's wings move. It can show what happens in the split second of a car crash. Super-slow motion can even show the flight of a speeding bullet.

Single-frame filming is used to show super-fast motion. The movie camera exposes just one frame at a time. It is used to show a speeded-up version of something that actually happened very slowly. For example, single-frame filming could show a bud opening into a flower. It actually took a week to open. But you could expose one frame of film every

two hours. At the end of the week, the film would be 84 frames long. Then, if you showed the film at 24 frames per second, the flower would open in just three and a half seconds. You can also use single-frame filming to make animated cartoons. (*See* **cartoon, animated.**)

Making a Movie Making a movie takes the skills of dozens of people. Most movies are filmed indoors on a *soundstage.* A soundstage is a large room or a building designed especially for making movies. It is soundproof so that microphones will not pick up any outside noises. There are no windows, so the amount of light can be controlled. A soundstage has plenty of space for people, cameras, lights, microphones, recording equipment, and scenery.

The *director of photography* is in charge of the camera operators. Several cameras may be filming at the same time. One may be filming from far away, a second from up close, and a third from above the actors.

The *sound director* carefully places the microphones to catch the voices of the actors and other sounds. Often a microphone is hung on a large rod and held above the actors, just out of sight of the camera. Many of the sounds you hear in movies are not made on the set or recorded on filming day. Special noises and background music are added later.

Special Effects One reason why movies can be so exciting is that they can show amazing—even impossible—things. Filmmakers have many ways of creating these special effects.

If there are scenes where the leading actor must jump from a moving car or hang by a rope from a helicopter, the director finds people with special skills to do this. They are dressed just the same as the leading actor, but they are experienced at doing dangerous tricks—called *stunts*—in the movies. (*See* **stuntmen and stuntwomen.**)

Other special effects use models. A huge spaceship exploding on the screen may really be a model spaceship exploding.

A favorite way to get special effects is to *superimpose* two different films—put one on top of the other. For example, a man is filmed running against a black background. Another film is made of a huge fire. When the two films are superimposed, it looks as though the man is running through the fire.

Special effects are also obtained with computer graphics. Computer programs can show the movement of planets or spaceships in a science-fiction movie, for example.

Sound directors also use special sound effects. A creaking door, footsteps on a dark street, rain, thunder, and many other noises can be added to the *sound track* of the movie after the shooting is done.

Videotape Moving pictures may also be recorded on videotape. Videotape is quite different from film. You cannot see the different frames on it. A video camera has lenses, like a movie camera. But a video camera translates the light it receives into electronic signals. These signals are recorded on the videotape.

Unlike film, videotape does not have to be developed. You can see the picture on a televison screen immediately after you have taken the tape from the video camera. Videotape can also be used again. You can record new images on a used videotape. These advantages make videotape popular for use at home and in school. (*See* **video recording.**)

See also **camera.**

A camera crew follows a movie actress on a horse. They push a dolly that has lights, camera, and a boom microphone to pick up what the character is saying.

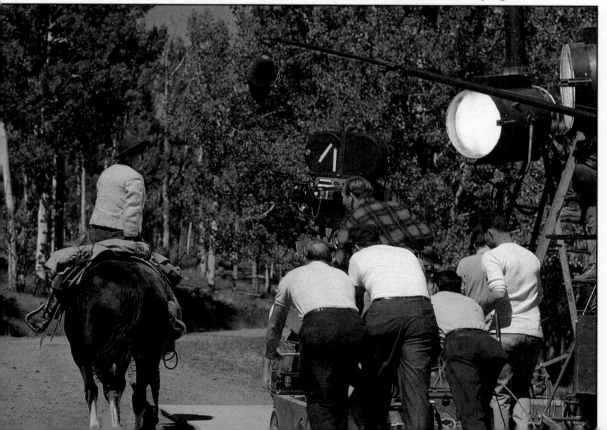

fingerprint

Look closely at the skin of your fingertips. You will see a pattern of ridges. When you touch something with dirty fingers, these ridges leave marks called *fingerprints*. Even when your hands are clean, the oil in your skin causes invisible fingerprints.

No two people, not even twins, have the same fingerprints. That is why we can use fingerprints to help identify people—war or accident victims, or even newborn babies in hospitals. We also use fingerprints to identify criminals. Smooth surfaces at the scene of a crime are dusted with powder. The powder sticks to the oil of the fingerprints, making them visible. Then the "prints" are lifted from the surface with sticky tape. Chemicals, too, can be used to make fingerprints visible.

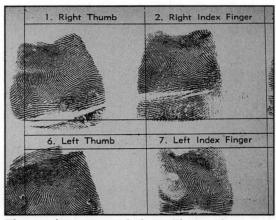

Fingerprints are made by rolling each finger in ink, then on paper.

There are four kinds of fingerprints. In a *loop pattern,* the ridges begin on one side of the fingertip, curve back sharply, and end on the same side. In a *whorl pattern,* the ridges form circles or spirals. In an *arch pattern,* the ridges cross from one side of the fingertip to the other, rising slightly in the center. An *accidental pattern* is a combination of loops, whorls, and arches.

Finland, *see* Europe

fiord

A fiord, or fjord, is a narrow valley with steep sides that has been flooded by the sea. Fiords are found along the mountainous shores of Alaska, Norway, Greenland, New Zealand, British Columbia, and southern Chile and Argentina.

During the last ice age, huge masses of ice called *glaciers* moved down mountain valleys to the sea. As they moved, the glaciers scraped away the rocky walls and floors of the valleys. This made the valleys into deep *gorges*—narrow valleys with very steep sides. Then, about 11,000 years ago, the earth began to warm again. The ice melted. The larger glaciers remained in the high mountains. The smaller ones melted away completely. The melted ice made sea levels rise. As the seas rose, they flooded the valleys that the glaciers had carved, forming the fiords. In this way, long, narrow arms of the sea invaded the land. (*See* **ice age.**)

The world's longest fiord, in eastern Greenland, extends almost 322 kilometers (200 miles) inland. Fiords are also very deep, so they make good natural harbors. In Norway, some fiords are as much as 1,219 meters (4,000 feet) deep.

See also **erosion** and **glacier.**

The waters of a Norwegian fiord are deep and cold.

A flame produces both heat and light. The brightest part is made by tiny pieces of carbon or soot that glow as they burn.

fire

Fire is the light and heat produced by a burning material. Materials burn when the substances they are made up of combine very quickly with oxygen.

Most materials we burn for fuel—such as wood, coal, and natural gas—contain carbon compounds. When one of these compounds *ignites*—bursts into flame—it produces a bluish light, steam, and heat. Tiny particles of black soot, which is mostly carbon, float above the blue flame. The heat makes the soot glow yellow and orange, producing most of the fire's light. Unburned soot is carried away by rising gases and forms the smoke. (*See* **carbon** and **compound**.)

There are several ways to start a fire without striking a match. You can rub two sticks together in some *tinder*—dry grass, leaves, or twigs. You can use a lens to focus sunlight on the tinder. You can strike a flint—a type of hard rock—against steel to create a spark. Matches were invented in 1827 by an English pharmacist, John Walker. He coated the tip of a stick with a mixture of chemicals. When the tip was quickly rubbed against a rough surface, heat from the friction ignited the chemicals. (*See* **match**.)

No one is sure how people first discovered fire and learned to control it. Early people certainly saw that lightning starts a fire and that striking two rocks together produces sparks. Once people could start and control

fire, survival became easier. People could live in colder areas and still keep warm. Fire gave warmth and light at night and during winter. Food could be cooked, and preserved by smoking. People used fire to shape metal tools and to harden pottery.

Fire was so necessary to early people that they thought of it as a gift from the gods. From earliest times, people worshiped fire. Ancient Egyptians, Greeks, Persians, and Romans built temples where sacred fires were kept burning. We still light candles for religious ceremonies, and build bonfires or set off fireworks for some holidays. The Olympic Flame that burns during the Olympic Games reminds us that fire still has special meaning for us.

Today, we use fire to warm our houses, to cook, and to generate electricity. Sparks help run the engines in our cars. Fire is used in factories to make steel and glass.

Fire is vital to our way of life. Yet fire can quickly get out of control. One match can start a fire that burns down an entire town. For this reason, you should never play with matches or candles.

See also **fire fighting**.

A blacksmith uses fire to soften metal so that he can shape it.

fire fighting

Fire performs many useful tasks, from heating our homes and cooking our food to propelling huge rockets into space. But when flames burn out of control, they cause destruction and even death. The job of fire fighting is as old as the discovery of fire itself. Thousands of years ago, when the first humans were learning how to make fire, they figured out ways to control it.

Fire Fighters   In America's early days, a fire brought neighbors running. They brought buckets and lined up in a chain called a *bucket brigade.* They passed buckets of water from a well or stream to the people trying to put out the fire.

Today, companies of fire fighters exist all over the United States. They form over 25,000 fire departments. Only about 1,000 of these departments hire professional fire fighters—people paid to fight fires.

Most fire departments are made up of volunteers who report to the firehouse or to the scene of a fire when needed. Some towns with volunteer companies hire one or more professionals to run the fire department.

Professional fire fighters live in the firehouse for a certain number of hours each week. During this time, they must always be ready to answer an alarm. Their shirts, pants, and knee-length coats are made of material that resists fire. Their helmets are made of leather with a wide brim that keeps

Fire fighters use trucks and ladders in cities. They use fireboats on water and planes to help put out forest fires.

water and falling objects away. An eye shield can be pulled down in front, and a chin strap keeps the helmet from being knocked off. Fire fighters' boots and gloves, too, are designed to protect them. Fire fighters may also wear masks to prevent them from breathing smoke from a fire.

Pumpers and Ladder Trucks   There are two main kinds of fire trucks. One is the *pumper,* which carries thousands of feet of hose. The hoses are between 1½ and 5 inches (3.75 and 12.5 centimeters) across. The pumper can be hooked up to a fire hydrant or a *standpipe*—a water pipe in a large building. A motor on the truck takes water from the hydrant or standpipe and pumps it through the hose. The pumper also has its own supply of several hundred gallons of water.

The other main kind of fire truck is the *ladder truck.* Some ladder trucks have an *aerial ladder.* When not in use, the ladder lies flat on the truck. At a fire, the ladder is automatically pulled out, much like a radio antenna. An aerial ladder may be 100 feet (30 meters) long, and reach as high as eight stories.

A second kind of ladder truck carries an *elevating platform.* This is a jointed *boom* with a "bucket" at the end. A boom is a long, armlike device that can be extended. A hose is usually built into the boom. Two or three people can fit into the bucket. Most elevating platforms are 75 to 100 feet (23 to 30.5 meters) long.

Both the aerial ladder and the elevating platform are mounted on a round turntable. This can turn the ladder in any direction.

A professional fire department in a big city is made up of several fire companies. The two main kinds of companies are *engine companies* and *ladder companies.* An engine company has one or more pumpers. A ladder company has one or more ladder trucks.

Other Equipment Fire departments, especially in big cities, may also use several other kinds of trucks. A *tender truck* carries extra hose and a small pump. A *rescue truck* carries fire-fighting tools, such as special torches for cutting through metal doors. It also carries fire-resistant suits and medical supplies. A *crash truck* serves airports and carries water or foam to spray on burning planes. A *fireboat* takes water from a lake or river and sprays it on burning boats or docks.

Fire-fighting trucks may be white, green, or any color that is easy to see. The color most often used is red.

Fighting a Fire in a City Building When a fire is reported to a city fire department, an official decides how many engine and ladder companies to send to the scene.

Each pumper and ladder truck usually carries five people. Everyone has a certain job to do. They connect the truck to the hydrant or standpipe, hook up the hose, control the pressure, and direct the water.

Members of the ladder company go into the building to see where the fire is. They look for people and rescue them if necessary. Fire fighters often use axes to break through walls and windows. This allows smoke and gas to escape the building.

Fighting Other Fires In the country, where there are no hydrants, fire fighters use the water carried by the pumper. If they are near a lake or river, they can draw water from it to pump through their hoses.

Forest and grassland fires are among the hardest to fight. The heat is often so great that trucks cannot get close. Fire fighters sometimes use airplanes or helicopters to drop chemicals on such fires. They may also create a *firebreak*—a strip of plowed or bulldozed land where there is nothing that can burn. When a fire reaches a firebreak, it cannot spread any farther.

Preventing Fires One of the most important ways to fight fires is to keep them from happening in the first place. Cities and towns have laws designed to help prevent fires. These may require the use of fireproof building materials. They may also require that whole buildings be inspected regularly for fire hazards. In many places, people are not allowed to burn their own trash or piles of dead leaves raked up in autumn.

You probably have been taught some fire safety rules. You may have been warned not to play with matches, and not to use the kitchen stove or build a campfire without an adult present. Wearing loose clothing near barbecue fires and stoves is very dangerous. Dishtowels and kitchen curtains should not come too close to a stove. Paints and other chemicals should be stored in cool places, in tightly sealed containers. Christmas tree lights should be carefully checked before use, and the trees themselves should not be allowed to dry out.

There are also rules about what to do if a fire starts. The first thing to do is call the fire department, because even a small fire can grow large very quickly. Schools, hospitals, and businesses have special exits, smoke alarms, and sprinkler systems in case of fire. They must have a plan to get everyone out of the building safely if a fire starts. That is why you have *fire drills* at school. Local fire departments advise families to have fire drills at home, too. Schools, hospitals, businesses, and sometimes homes have *fire extinguishers*—special red tanks with nozzles on top that can squirt a liquid or a dry powder to *extinguish*—put out—the fire.

WHAT SHOULD YOU DO IN CASE OF FIRE?

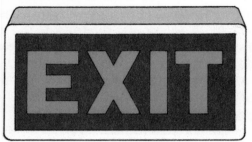

BE READY:

At home, think about which doors or windows you could safely use in an emergency.

In school, know where the exits are, and where you should go in case of fire.

In an auditorium or theater, look around for the exits. They are marked with exit signs.

ACT QUICKLY:

Leave the area of the fire immediately.

When you are safely away, call the fire department or get other help.

If a grown-up is in charge, follow directions.

DO NOT PANIC:

Do not run or push others.

DO NOT open doors that feel warm or are letting in smoke around their edges.

If there is heavy smoke, get down on the floor. The air there may be better for breathing.

If you cannot get out immediately, call for help and keep calling until help comes.

firefly

Fireflies are not flies. They are beetles. There are more than 1,000 different kinds of fireflies in the world.

Fireflies are often called *lightning bugs.* All fireflies produce light. The light is made by five chemicals in the firefly's body. Some produce continuous light. Others produce

A male firefly has wings. He uses his light to send signals to the female.

flashes of light. In some tropical countries, people put many fireflies into a bottle and use the bottle as a lantern!

The purpose of the light is to attract a mate. A male uses different patterns of flashes to let the female fireflies know which kind he is.

Fireflies rest during the day and are active at night. Most of the fireflies that fly through the night sky are males. Female fireflies usually do not have wings and are sometimes called *glowworms*. They sit on bushes and trees. They signal back to male fireflies to show where they are. Some kinds of female fireflies can fly. They imitate the signals of other kinds of females to attract males. Then they eat them.

Most female fireflies do not have wings. They are often called glowworms.

Firefly *larvae* — young fireflies — hatch from eggs. The larvae look like little worms and may produce light. If they do, they may be called glowworms, too. They pass through a resting stage before they change into adults. (*See* **larva**.)

first aid

First aid is the immediate care given to the victim of an accident or sudden illness. First aid can save a person's life. It can also prevent permanent injuries.

There are some general rules that you should follow when giving first aid.

Think Before You Act First, think through the situation. Decide what you can do to help. Do not try to give treatment if you are confused about what to do. Others may be present who know more about first aid than you do. Whoever knows the most should be in charge.

If you are alone, you must treat any life-threatening conditions before going for help. Remove a victim from a fire, from water, or from fumes or smoke.

Every home should keep a list of emergency numbers near the telephone. If you cannot find them, call the operator for help.

There are a number of places where you can take lessons in first aid. The American Red Cross gives first-aid classes. Many youth organizations, such as the scouts and 4-H clubs, have classes, too. If you learn first aid, you will be better prepared to help relieve suffering and even save lives.

WHOM TO CALL IN AN EMERGENCY

If there is an emergency, you need to know how to get help. These phone numbers should be near a phone in every home. Before you call, take a few seconds to decide whom to call first. Making the right choice could be very important.

OPERATOR (DIAL 0)
PARENT
NEIGHBOR
GENERAL EMERGENCY
POLICE
FIRE
AMBULANCE
POISON CONTROL CENTER
DOCTOR
CHILDREN'S DOCTOR
DENTIST
VETERINARIAN

FIRST AID

Bleeding Most wounds stop bleeding by themselves. You should just wash a small cut with soap and water. Be sure that any dirt has been removed. A prepared bandage may be placed over the cut.

Severe wounds will not stop bleeding unless you apply pressure to them. Have the victim lie down. Place the wounded part above the rest of the body if possible. Place a clean cloth over the wound and press firmly with your hand. If you have no cloth, press on the wound with your hand. If the victim bleeds through the first cloth, place another on top

of it and press more firmly. When the bleeding has stopped, tie the cloth over the wound.

A nosebleed is a special case. To stop a nosebleed, pinch the nose closed. After a while, the bleeding will stop.

Blows to the Head A blow to the head can knock a person unconscious. Get the victim to a doctor as soon as possible. Even if the blow does not cause unconsciousness, watch the victim closely for other signs. For example, the victim may have difficulty walking or talking, or double vision. If these signs appear, see a doctor.

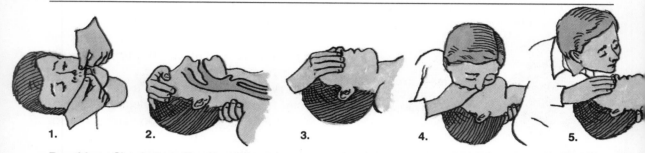

1. 2. 3. 4. 5.

Breathing Six minutes without breathing can cause death. If the victim's chest stops moving and the skin and tongue turn blue, try to restore breathing at once.

The best way to restore breathing is to use mouth-to-mouth resuscitation. 1. Place the victim on his or her back. Kneel down near the head. Remove any objects from the mouth. 2. Place one hand under the victim's neck and the other hand on the forehead. Tilt the head so that the chin points upward. This position opens the airway. 3. Pinch the nostrils shut with the hand that is on the forehead. 4. Take a deep breath. Cover the open mouth tightly with your own. Blow hard enough to make the chest rise. 5. Remove your mouth and listen for the air coming out. Repeat this every five seconds.

To treat an infant, place your mouth over both the mouth and nose. Blow gently, remove your mouth, and listen for the air coming out. Repeat every three seconds.

Burns Treatment for burns depends on how severe they are. Burns that cause redness and blisters should be placed in cool water to relieve the pain. Burns that destroy layers of the skin should be covered with a clean dressing. A doctor should examine all serious burns.

Choking Choking can occur if food or an object gets stuck in the throat. A person who is choking cannot breathe or talk. Death can result if the object is not removed.

The Heimlich maneuver is a good way to remove the object. Grasp the victim around the body and squeeze sharply just under the breastbone. This forces air out of the lungs and blows the object out of the throat.

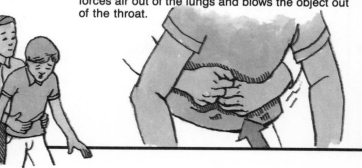

Fractures and Dislocations   Victims of automobile and sports accidents often have fractures and dislocations. A fracture is a break in a bone. A dislocation is a bone forced out of its joint. Fractures and dislocations cause pain and swelling.

Keep the victim quiet and treat for shock. Try not to move a broken bone or dislocated joint. Moving can damage nerves, muscles, and blood vessels. Do not move a person who may have a broken neck or back. Moving the victim could cause death.

Heart attacks   Heart attacks are among the leading causes of death. Most heart attacks begin with an intense pain across the chest. The pain spreads to the neck, arms, and stomach. It usually lasts about five minutes. The victim may find it hard to breathe and may feel like vomiting. Call a doctor or ambulance at once. Do not allow the victim to move. If the victim's heart stops beating, a treatment called CPR can be used. CPR (cardiopulmonary resuscitation) should be done only by someone who is trained.

There are a number of places where you can take lessons in first aid, including CPR. The American Red Cross gives first-aid classes. Many youth organizations, such as the scouts and 4-H clubs, have classes, too. If you learn first aid, you will be better prepared to help relieve suffering and even save lives.

Poisoning   There are two kinds of treatment for poisoning. The poison can be removed from the body, or an *antidote* can be given. An antidote is a substance that acts against the poison.

First, look for the poison that was swallowed. The label on the container may tell you what to do in case of poisoning. You can also ask the telephone operator to connect you with a *poison control center* to ask for help. If the victim is awake, give the antidote at once. Do *not* give it if the victim is unconscious. Instead, make sure the person can breathe.

If you do not know what the victim has swallowed, you will not know what the correct antidote is. In that case, have the victim swallow plenty of water or milk to dilute the poison. Again, do this only if the victim is conscious.

For some poisons, it is helpful if the victim vomits. That removes poison from the stomach. In other cases, however, the victim should *not* vomit. Do not make the victim vomit if he or she is unconscious. Do not make the victim vomit if he or she has swallowed harsh chemicals that cause burns, or petroleum products such as gasoline.

To make a person vomit, use a drug called *syrup of ipecac*, which is found in many first-aid kits. If you do not have any syrup of ipecac, press your finger at the back of the victim's throat. When the victim begins to vomit, lay the person on the stomach with the head hanging down. This will prevent the poisoned vomit from getting into the lungs.

In all cases, get the victim to a hospital as quickly as possible.

Shock   Shock results when the blood is not circulating properly. Any serious injury or illness can cause shock. A person in shock may feel very weak. The skin is pale and damp. The heart beats quickly. Breathing is quick and shallow, or deep and uneven.

To treat shock, place the victim on his or her back and raise the legs slightly. Put blankets over and under the body to keep the victim warm.

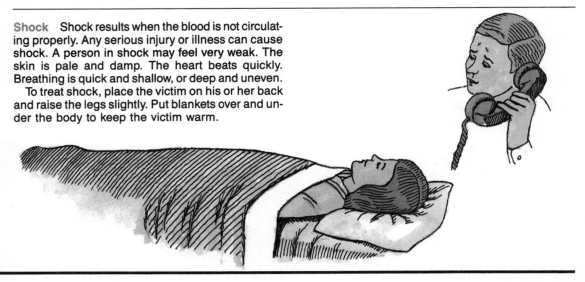

fish

Wherever there is water, there are fish. Fish live in oceans, ponds, rivers, wells, caves, and marshes. They live in icy polar seas and warm tropical bays. They live in sunny mountain lakes and underground streams. Some, such as goldfish, live as pets in people's homes.

There are more than 26,000 known kinds of fish. They come in many different sizes, colors, and shapes. The smallest, a pygmy goby that lives in the Philippines, is only 1.2 centimeters (1/2 inch) long. The largest, the whale shark, may grow to more than 15 meters (50 feet) in length. Luckily, this giant shark is harmless.

Fish come in black, white, and every color of the rainbow. Some fish, including many kinds that live in coral reefs, have brilliant colors and patterns. Others are dull grays or browns. Most fish have streamlined bodies. This makes it easier for them to move through the water. Eels are long and skinny. But many fish that live on the ocean floor, such as flounders and skates, are flat. Puffers can blow up to look like round balloons. The sea horse hardly looks like a fish at all.

What Is a Fish?   All fish are alike in important ways. All are *vertebrates.* They have backbones, which are made up of many bones called *vertebrae.* At the front end, the backbone is connected to the skull, which contains the brain.

If you pick up a fish, you get slime on your hands. This slime is called *mucus.* Mucus keeps the skin moist. It also protects the fish against bacteria and other germs.

Most fish have an outer covering made of *scales.* Usually, the scales overlap one another, like shingles on a roof. Scales protect the fish. A puffer has scales with long spines. The spines stick out when the fish puffs up.

Fish are *cold-blooded.* This means that their body temperature is about the same as the water in which they live. People can keep their body temperature constant, even though the temperature outdoors varies. Fish cannot. A fish living in the Arctic has cold blood. A fish living in the tropics has warm blood. If the water temperature suddenly changes, the fish in that water will die.

All fish need oxygen. Without oxygen, they suffocate and die. A few fish have structures similar to our lungs. They can breathe air. But most fish get oxygen from the water. As they swim, they take in water through the mouth. The water flows over their *gills,* which remove the oxygen. Carbon dioxide and other wastes pass from the gills into the water. Then the water passes out through openings in the side of the head.

Blood flows through the gills. It picks up the oxygen and carries it to other parts of the fish's body. The blood also takes wastes from the body cells and carries them to the gills. Like all vertebrates, a fish has a heart. A fish heart has two chambers. One chamber collects blood coming from the back part of the

Three strange saltwater fish: When the puffer puffs up, sharp spines stick out to protect it. The sea horse "stands" head-up. The ray has huge, winglike fins.

spotted eagle ray

bandtail puffer

dwarf sea horse

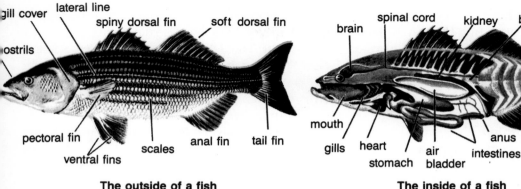

The outside of a fish

gill cover
lateral line
spiny dorsal fin
soft dorsal fin
nostrils
pectoral fin
ventral fins
scales
anal fin
tail fin

The inside of a fish

brain
spinal cord
kidney
backbone
mouth
gills
heart
stomach
air bladder
intestines
anus
muscles

body. The other chamber pumps the blood forward, to the head and gills.

How Fish Move Almost every fish swims by moving its tail from side to side. This pushes the fish forward. Fins on the fish's body are used for steering and braking. They also keep the fish upright. Most fish have two pairs of fins. One pair are the *pectoral fins.* They are behind the head, one on each side. The second pair are the *pelvic fins.* They are on the belly of the fish. Fish also have a single *dorsal fin* that runs down the center of the back. A single *anal fin* is on the belly, just in front of the tail.

A few fish can "fly" or walk. The flying fish has huge pectoral fins. When it leaves the water, it extends these fins and glides through the air. It may cover several hundred feet before returning to the water.

The mudskipper has thick pectoral fins. It can use these like legs to walk onto land. It climbs onto rocks or moves across mud flats and sand at low tide. Batfish and lizard fish

**Some fish move in interesting ways:
A remora hitches rides on a shark.
A lizardfish walks along the seafloor.
A flying fish can sail through the air.**

live on the bottom of the sea. They use their thick fins to walk along the ocean floor.

The pectoral fins of a skate are called "wings." The skate doesn't use its tail for swimming. It uses its pectoral fins. As a skate moves through the water, it flaps its fins just like a bird flaps its wings during flight.

Many fish have a *swim bladder* in their bodies. This is a sac filled with gas. When the fish wants to go deeper in the water, it empties the swim bladder. This makes the fish heavier. When the fish wants to rise, it fills the bladder with gas. Since gas is light, this makes the fish lighter.

Sense Organs Fish get information from the environment through their sense organs. These include eyes, ears, and organs of taste and smell. The fish also has a system called the *lateral line* that is sensitive to vibrations in the water.

Atlantic flying fish

red lizard fish

shark

remora

Most fish have good eyesight. Like us, they have two eyes. But both eyes do not face ahead like ours. They have one eye on each side of the head. So the two eyes do not look at the same thing at the same time. The two eyes see different images. This gives the fish a large field of vision. The fish can see what is ahead, behind, above, and below. Fish do not have eyelids. They have to sleep with their eyes open.

Fish ears also are different from human ears. Fish do not have outside ears, as we do. They have only internal ears. Their two ears pick up sounds and are important for balance. The inner ears let the fish know its direction in the water. For example, they let the fish know if its head is up or down.

People have taste buds in their mouths. Some fish have taste buds all over their bodies! Taste is very important to fish, because it helps the fish find food. Smell also is important, especially to sharks and other predators—fish that eat other animals.

The lateral line is found only in fish. It is made up of special cells arranged in a line along each side of the head and body. The lateral line is sensitive to pressure and vibrations. It lets the fish know where unseen fish and animals are. It also helps the fish judge how far it is from rocks and other objects. This is very useful for fish that live in dark or muddy waters. One cave-dwelling fish uses its lateral line to pick up vibrations that are made by tiny animals swimming through the water. The vibrations tell the fish where the animals are, so it can catch and eat them.

Many fish that live far below the ocean's surface have body structures that produce light. The light has many purposes. Some of these fish use the light to advertise for mates, to keep groups of fish together, or to frighten predators. Some use light as bait, to attract prey—the animals they eat.

How Fish Get Food Fish eat many different foods—and have many different ways of getting food. Some are predators. Most predators have strong jaws and sharp teeth. Bluefish, barracuda, tuna, and most sharks are predators that chase and eat other fish. The sea bream is a predator that eats clams and related shellfish. It has large teeth in its throat that crush the shells.

Some predators have very unusual ways of catching their dinner. The anglerfish has a spine on top of its head. The spine has a fleshy tip. Other fish see this and think it is something to eat. When they get close enough, the anglerfish grabs them with its sharp teeth.

The archerfish is another unusual hunter. It catches insects that live near the water. The archerfish shoots water at the insects. When the water hits an insect on a branch, the insect falls down. If it lands in the water, the archerfish eats it.

Other fish are plant-eaters. Parrot fish have teeth that form a beak. They use the beak to scrape algae off rocks. One kind of catfish uses its lips as suckers to attach itself to rocks. Then it snips algae off the rocks.

Some fish get food in clever ways. The archerfish shoots water at insects. The parrotfish scrapes algae off rocks. The anglerfish attracts fish with a "lure" so that it can catch and eat them.

archerfish

blue parrot fish

Pipefish are protected from enemies because they look like the sea plants they live in.

Whale sharks and herring are examples of filter feeders. They take in large gulps of water and filter out—remove—tiny plants and animals. Near the back of the mouth, whale sharks and herring have comblike structures called *gill rakers.* These filter out the food as the water passes by. Then the fish swallows the food.

How Fish Protect Themselves Many fish have colors that blend with the colors of their environment. This protects the fish. It makes it difficult for prey and enemies to see them. Flounders, soles, and groupers are among the fish that can change their colors to match the environment.

Several fish protect themselves by looking like other objects. Stonefish look like stones. Pipefish look like the long leaves of the grass they live among. They can stay in a vertical

The sawtooth can slash at enemies with its sawlike teeth. Other fish, such as the stonefish and the flounder, protect themselves by being hard to see.

position—head up or tail up—for long periods of time. (*See* **camouflage.**)

Some other fish have weapons or armor. The sawfish has a long snout that looks like a double-edged saw. It uses this to defend itself and to attack prey. Many fish have sharp spines. In some fish, the spines are connected to glands that produce poison. The dogfish has a sharp spine in front of each of its two back fins. A painful poison is given off by glands connected to the spines. If an enemy grabs a dogfish, the dogfish will twist and bend its body so its spines can slash and poison the enemy. Lionfish and stonefish also have sharp spines and poison glands.

The entire body of the boxfish, except the fins, is covered by a spiny coat of armor. The spines can cause terrible wounds. Very few predators attack a boxfish. But if they do manage to eat a boxfish, they still lose, because the meat of the boxfish is poisonous.

Some fish protect themselves by shocking their enemies. Certain catfish, rays, and other fish can generate electricity. They use this electricity to stun or kill enemies. These fish also use the electricity to catch food and to find their way through the water. (*See* **electric fish.**)

The remora, or suckerfish, has a disk on the top of its head. The remora uses the disk to attach itself to sharks and other large fish. Being with a large fish protects the remora from its enemies. There are other advantages, too. The remora can eat bits of food left over from its host's meals. And it gets a free ride to new feeding grounds.

smalltooth sawfish

stonefish

summer flounder

anglerfish

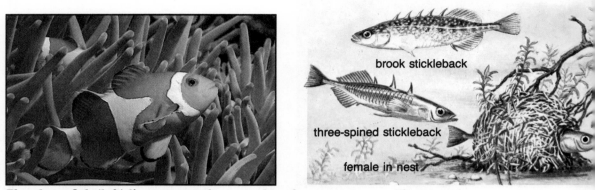

brook stickleback

three-spined stickleback

female in nest

The clown fish (left) lives among the tentacles of a sea anemone. The tentacles are poisonous to most other fish. Sticklebacks (right) make nests to lay their eggs in.

Brightly colored clownfish often live among the tentacles of sea anemones. The tentacles have stinging cells that are poisonous to other fish. But they do not hurt the clownfish. By living among the tentacles, the clownfish are protected from predators. The sea anemones are helped, too. The clownfish eat wastes that collect on the anemones' tentacles. They may also help the sea anemone get food. Other fish try to catch the clownfish. Instead, the predators are caught and eaten by the sea anemones.

Many fish live in groups called *schools.* This protects individual fish against hungry enemies. All the fish in a school are of the same kind. Schools come in different sizes. A school of tuna has about 20 fish. A school of herring has several thousand fish.

The Life Cycle of Fish Almost all fish hatch from eggs. The young fish usually do not look like their parents. They are called *larvae.* Gradually, they *metamorphose*— change—into adults. A few fish, such as the guppy and platy, give birth to live larvae.

Some fish—such as sharks and guppies—produce young by mating. The male fish deposits sperm inside the female to fertilize her eggs. Most fish do not mate. The male fertilizes the eggs after the female lays them. The female lays many eggs. A female cod may lay 100 million eggs! Most of the eggs will die or be eaten. Most of the larvae that hatch will also die or be eaten. The life of a young fish is filled with danger. Perhaps only two or three of the 100 million eggs will eventually become adult cod.

Some fish make nests for their eggs. They lay fewer eggs. But the eggs are protected by

Many small fish live in large groups called *schools.* Staying together protects individual fish from other creatures who might want to catch and eat them.

the nest and have a greater chance of hatching. Even better protection is given by the male pipefish. He has a pouch on his belly. The female puts her eggs into the pouch. After the young pipefish hatch, their father takes care of them until they are old enough to manage for themselves.

Scientists are not sure exactly how long different fish live. Some small fish may live for only a year. Carp may live 50 years in people's garden pools. But very few fish die of old age. Most are caught by predators or die of disease.

Kinds of Fish There are three main groups of fish: jawless fish, cartilage fish, and bony fish.

Lampreys and hagfish are the only jawless fish. They do not have jaws, real teeth, paired fins, or scales. The skeleton is made of cartilage instead of bone. Cartilage is softer than bone. (Your ear and the tip of your nose are made of cartilage.) Lampreys and hagfish have long, slimy bodies. The mouth is a sucker. Many lampreys are vampires. They attach themselves to other fish and suck their victims' blood.

Sharks, skates, and rays are cartilage fish. Their skeletons are made of cartilage. But they have jaws, teeth, and paired fins. Their bodies are covered with scales. The scales are like tiny teeth. If you ran your hand over the body of a shark, it would feel like rough sandpaper. No cartilage fish has a swim bladder. (*See* **bone.**)

Almost all fish are bony fish. Their skeletons are made of bone. They have jaws, teeth, and paired fins. Their scales are thin plates covered by a thin layer of skin. Their bodies feel much smoother than the body of a cartilage fish. Almost all bony fish have a swim bladder.

People and Fish Since earliest times, people all over the world have caught and eaten fish. Fishing is a major industry and a popular sport in all parts of the world. Fish farming is important, too. Fish farmers raise trout, catfish, and other tasty fish in special ponds called "farms." (*See* **fishing.**)

Many people keep fish as pets in aquariums and outdoor pools. People also like to go skin diving so they can watch fish in their natural environment. (*See* **aquarium** and **diving.**)

A few fish can be dangerous. Sharks and piranha sometimes attack people, and certain fish, such as puffers, are poisonous if eaten. Barracuda, parrot fish, and some sea bass may also be poisonous.

See also **eel; goldfish; piranha; salmon; sea horse; shark;** and **tropical fish.**

fishing

For thousands of years, people have caught and eaten animals that live in rivers, lakes, or the sea. We catch these animals by fishing for them. We "fish" not only for fish but also for hard-shelled mollusks such as clams, for crustaceans such as shrimp, and for certain water mammals, such as porpoises.

In almost every part of the world, there are people who earn their living from the sea. They catch fish and other water animals in order to feed themselves, and they sell the rest for profit. Other people go fishing just for fun.

There are two main ways of catching fish: by hooking them on a line, or by catching them in nets.

Fishing is both a sport and an important way of getting food.

fishing

Hook-and-Line Fishing When we think of fishing, we usually think of using a hook and line. This is the method used by people for sport or to catch a few fish for dinner. Bait is placed on a metal hook that is attached to a long line. The bait may be real food that the fish might eat, such as a worm or small fish. Or it may be artificial bait—imitation fish food made from feathers, plastic, or metal. You *cast*—throw—the line out into the water, usually by means of a fishing pole or rod. If a fish nibbles at the bait, it may get the hook stuck in its mouth. To bring in the fish, you quickly turn a reel that winds up the line.

For commercial fishing, many fishing lines with dangling hooks are connected and set out in large lakes or the ocean. The entire line can be hauled in for a big catch.

Fishing with Nets There are three ways to catch fish with nets. The first way is called simply *netting*. It has been used to haul in large quantities of fish off the coasts of every

These fishermen are using nets to catch fish in Mexico.

continent. In the small fishing villages of Asia, Africa, and South America, setting the nets is an important job.

Nets of different shapes are used in different parts of the world. Mexican fisherman use "butterfly nets" to catch lake fish. Phillipine fishermen use smaller skimming nets to catch pond fish.

The net is made with holes just a little smaller than the fish to be caught. Small

Sport fishermen use lures called *flies* (right) to catch fish.

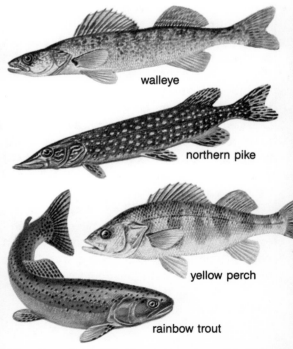

walleye

northern pike

yellow perch

rainbow trout

floats sewn into the net keep it afloat. Underwater, the nets are hard to see. A fish swimming toward one may become stuck by its gills. When the net is hauled in, there may be thousands of fish in it.

The first fish nets were made by hand from natural fibers, such as cotton and grasses. Much time was spent making new nets and repairing old ones. Today, most nets are made of fine strands of plastic.

Seining is a second way of fishing with nets. It is done by encircling the fish in a net

Many freshwater fish (left) are fun to catch and good to eat. Saltwater fish such as tuna and mackerel are important as a source of food in many parts of the world.

bluefin tuna

chub mackerel

Atlantic sailfish

bag known as a *seine.* Seine netting has holes much smaller than the fish to be caught. When the seine is thrown overboard, the fish swim into it. Then the seine is closed, and the fish are hauled in.

Trawling is a third method of fishing with nets. It is used by commercial fishing boats that go out to sea for tons of fish. These boats, called *trawlers,* drag along huge net bags similar to seines. They collect all the fish that enter the open end. The fish caught depends on the net's size, shape, and depth.

This method of fishing goes back to ancient Egypt. A pair of trawlers would fish together with the net between them. Today, commercial boats trawl to catch bottom-dwelling flatfish. Other boats trawl the Gulf of Mexico for shrimp.

Other Methods Some other tools for fishing include fishing baskets, rakes for combing the sand for shellfish, traps to catch lobsters, and tongs to get oysters out of their beds. For large fish, fishing spears and harpoons are used.

Protecting Water Animals Modern fishing is so efficient that it threatens some water animals with extinction. Ships have radar that can locate large schools of fish. They also have huge nets that can scoop up tons of fish at once.

Many boats are floating fish factories. The fish are cleaned, sorted, packaged, and frozen ready for the market. If fish are frozen on the boat, large fishing boats can stay out longer and catch tons more fish before coming back to land. These practices can take all the fish from one area away quickly.

To protect this valuable source of food, nations now have laws about which areas may be fished and how many fish may be caught. Worldwide organizations keep the fishing industry informed about limits and about where and when fish are breeding. These are important conservation measures.

See also **fish.**

fjord, *see* **fiord**

flag

A flag can be described simply as a piece of cloth having certain colors and designs. A flag is more than that, however, because it is also a symbol. A flag can stand for a nation, like the United States. It can stand for a state, such as California. A flag can also stand for a person or an organization. The president of the United States has a special flag. So do the Scouts, the Olympic Games, and the Red Cross. Many schools and colleges have their own flags, too.

School pennants are triangular flags.

How Flags Developed The first flags were probably used in China about 3,000 years ago. Whenever the Chinese ruler went out in public, someone would carry a white flag in front of him. It was so sacred that anyone who even touched the flagbearer was punished.

Flags were important in warfare. An officer could see how his troops were doing on the battlefield by watching their flags. When soldiers fought with bows and arrows, flags were used to show which way the wind was blowing. This helped archers aim properly. If soldiers captured the enemy army's flag, it often meant the battle was over.

Signal flags are sometimes used by armies and navies to send messages. These flags are of various colors, and are held in different positions to indicate letters or words. Signal flags were more commonly used before radio was invented. They are still used today when there is a chance that the enemy might be listening in.

National Flags Every nation has its own flag. A flag helps inspire *patriotism*—love of country. It is such a powerful symbol that when people want to show hatred of a country, they will often burn its flag.

Most national flags use at least two of seven colors: red, white, blue, green, yellow, black, and orange. A flag's color often has a special meaning. The red of the Soviet Union's flag is a symbol of the 1917 revolution that brought the Communists to power. The combination of red, yellow, and green symbolizes African unity. These colors appear in the flags of Ethiopia, Ghana, and other African countries.

One of the most common designs for a flag is three broad stripes or bands. These are arranged either across the flag (horizontally), or up and down (vertically). Often, one of the bands will contain a design. For example, the Canadian flag has a red band on either side of the flag, and a white band in between with a big red maple leaf in the middle of it.

Rwanda

Nepal

Canada

The flag of India has horizontal orange, white, and green bands. In the middle of the white band is the Wheel of the Law, an ancient Indian symbol.

A nation's flag often tells a story about its history. The flag of Great Britain, is a combination of the flags used by England, Scotland, and Ireland before they united. The British flag also appears on the flag of Australia. Below it is a large star, which symbolizes the British Commonwealth of Nations, to which Australia belongs. There is also a group of five stars on the flag. They represent the *constellation*—star cluster—called the Southern Cross, which can be seen in the sky over Australia.

1777 · 1814 · 1818 · 1846 · 1912-1959 · U.S. flag of today

The U.S. flag changed as new states joined the Union. Today it has 50 stars, one for each state, and 13 stripes, one for each of the original states.

The flag of Saudi Arabia is unusual because it is one of the few that has words. Written in white on a green background are Arabic words saying, "There is no God but Allah, and Muhammad is His Prophet." This is the most important teaching of the Islamic religion, which began in Saudi Arabia.

Another unusual flag is that of Nepal, a small country in Asia. Nepal's flag is the only

Australia

Saudi Arabia

one in the world not shaped like a rectangle. Instead, it is made up of two triangles, one above the other. In the top triangle is a moon, and in the lower triangle is a sun.

The Flag of the United States The red-white-and-blue flag of the United States is known as "Old Glory" or the "Stars and Stripes." When Americans sing "The Star-Spangled Banner," they are singing about their country's flag. Americans also honor their flag and country when they recite the Pledge of Allegiance.

In 1777, during the Revolutionary War, members of the Continental Congress decided on a design for the American flag. The flag would have 13 stripes, red alternating with white. These would represent the

American colonies. Thirteen white stars on a blue background would serve as a symbol of a new country, or as Congress stated, "a new constellation." Red stood for courage, white for purity, and blue for justice. (*See* **Ross, Betsy.**)

At first, whenever a new state joined the Union, a new stripe and a new star was added to the flag. In 1818, however, Congress decided to keep 13 stripes as a reminder of the original colonies, and to add a new star every time a state joined the Union.

Most countries have special rules about how their flags should be used. In the United States, the flag may be displayed outdoors from sunrise to sunset. It is often lowered to *half-mast*—halfway between the top and bottom of the flagpole—when a national hero dies. Hanging it upside down is a distress signal—a call for help. The flag is never allowed to touch the ground.

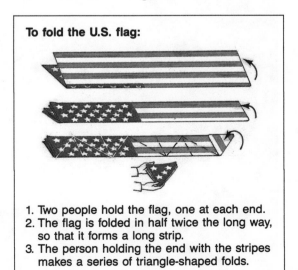

To fold the U.S. flag:

1. Two people hold the flag, one at each end.
2. The flag is folded in half twice the long way, so that it forms a long strip.
3. The person holding the end with the stripes makes a series of triangle-shaped folds.

Fleming, Sir Alexander

Sir Alexander Fleming was a British scientist. In 1928, he discovered the first drug that could kill bacteria in the body without harming humans.

Fleming had been looking for such a drug. He was growing bacteria on plates for his experiments. By chance, some mold landed on one of his plates. To his surprise, Fleming noticed that bacteria did not grow near the mold. The mold made something that stopped the bacteria from growing. Fleming named the substance *penicillin*. When he tested penicillin on human tissue, he found that it did not cause harm.

In order to use penicillin as a drug, it had to be separated from the mold and purified. Fleming could not find a way to do this. In the late 1930s, two British scientists, Ernst Chain and Howard Florey, found a way to produce pure penicillin. In 1940, the first patient was treated successfully with penicillin. He was a British policeman who had blood poisoning.

Fleming's discovery opened a new era for medicine. In 1945, Fleming, Florey, and Chain won the Nobel Prize in Medicine for their work with penicillin.

See also **drugs and medicines; antibiotic; bacteria;** and **mold.**

flood

A flood is an overflow of water that covers what is usually dry land. Floods can be major disasters. They can carry away animals, people, trees, soil, cars, and even buildings. In 1887, at least 900,000 people drowned when China's Huang He river flooded.

Most rainwater and melted snow soaks into the ground. The rest runs off the land into streams and rivers. When there is a great deal of rain, snow, or melting ice, too much water may pour into rivers and streams. They overflow their banks and flood the surrounding land.

Some floods, called *flash floods,* give little warning. Eastern Colorado's Big Thompson River winds down a narrow canyon. Usually,

A flood drove these people out of their homes. Helping agencies provided them with food and shelter. Governments look for ways to prevent dangerous floods.

These cranberry farmers flood fields
on purpose to help harvest the berries.

it is a fast-moving mountain stream about
60 centimeters (2 feet) deep. On July 31,
1976, more than 30 centimeters (12 inches)
of rain fell. The Big Thompson River quickly
overflowed its banks. Torrents of water—
in some places 9 meters (29½ feet)
deep—roared down the canyon. It swept
away houses, restaurants, and bridges. It
smashed cars against the sides of the rocky
canyon. In this flash flood, 139 people died.

In Egypt, the Nile River used to flood every
year. For centuries, it left behind rich soil
picked up on its long journey from central
Africa. This soil made the plain around the
Nile one of the world's most fertile farming
regions. In 1970, the Aswan High Dam was
built to stop the Nile from flooding. The res-
ervoir behind the dam stores water for use
during dry seasons. Unfortunately, without
the floods, no new soil reaches the plain.
Farmers must now fertilize their soil.

Dams are often built to prevent flooding.
But if dams burst, they can cause disastrous
flash floods. On June 9, 1972, a downpour
soaked Rapid City, South Dakota. In six
hours, 35 centimeters (13½ inches) of rain
fell. On the outskirts of town, an earthen
dam controlled the flow of Rapid Creek. That
night, the dam broke. A wall of water surged
through Rapid City. It destroyed 1,200
homes and took 237 lives. (*See* **dam**.)

The ocean can also cause floods, usually
pushed by high winds. Hurricanes whip up
gigantic ocean waves that batter the sea-
coast. In 1970, a huge wall of water swept
over the coastline of East Pakistan. More
than 500,000 people died. (*See* **hurricane**.)

Earthquakes, volcanoes, and landslides
sometimes create gigantic waves called *tsunamis*. The waves may rush across the
ocean at speeds of 1,000 kilometers (620
miles) per hour. When they approach land,
they pile up into monstrous walls of water,
15 to 30 meters (49 to 98 feet) high. In 1883,
a tsunami caused by the eruption of Kraka-
toa volcano killed 37,000 people in Java and
Sumatra. (*See* **earthquake** and **volcano**.)

In many countries, people have built sea-
walls to prevent flooding. In the Netherlands,
they have constructed dikes to keep out the
North Sea. From time to time, dikes and sea-
walls fail. Disastrous floods have resulted.
(*See* **dikes and levees**.)

The National Weather Service warns people when hurricanes, tsunamis, and river
flooding are expected. The best protection is
to seek high ground until it is over.

See also **disaster**.

Florida

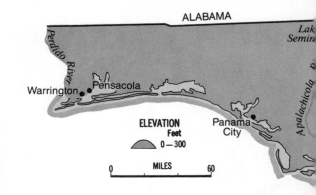

Florida

Capital: Tallahassee
Area: 58,664 square miles (151,940 square kilometers) (22nd-largest state)
Population (1980): 9,739,992 (1985): about 11,366,000 (6th-largest state)
Became a state: March 3, 1845 (27th state)

Florida is a state in the southeastern corner of the United States. Millions of people come to Florida every year to visit Disney World, the Kennedy Space Center, and Everglades National Park. They are also attracted by the beaches along Florida's long shoreline.

Because of its beautiful weather, Florida is known as the "Sunshine State." More retired people move to Florida than to any other state. Nearly one person in every five in Florida is 65 years old or more. Florida is also the home of many Cuban Americans.

Land Most of Florida is a *peninsula*—an arm of land surrounded by water on three sides. It extends between the Atlantic Ocean and the Gulf of Mexico. North of the peninsula is a long strip of land that stretches west. It is called the Panhandle.

The Everglades, a giant swamp, covers much of the southern end of the Florida peninsula. The Florida Keys, a group of small islands off the southern tip of Florida, extend into the Gulf of Mexico. Florida also has many rivers, streams, and lakes. Lake Okeechobee is the largest lake in the southeastern United States. (*See* **Everglades.**)

Florida is very flat. The highest point in the state is only 345 feet (105 meters) above sea level. The flat land and good climate have made Florida an important farming state. It is famous for its citrus fruits. Packing plants produce millions of servings of fresh and frozen orange juice each day. Florida's farms also produce vegetables, cotton, tobacco, sugarcane, peanuts, and tomatoes. Fishing, mining, manufacturing, and tourism are other important industries.

People Florida is one of the fastest growing states. Each year, thousands more people move to Florida from colder areas in the U.S. and Canada. Most settle in or near cities. The state's largest urban area is Miami, on the Atlantic shore near the state's southern tip. Two other large urban regions are the area around Tampa-St. Petersburg on Florida's west coast, and the Fort Lauderdale-Hollywood area, north of Miami.

The city of Orlando is in the central part of the state. It is near Disney World and other tourist attractions. Jacksonville is the largest city in northern Florida. It has an area of 760 square miles (1,968 square kilometers)—larger than any other city in the United States.

History The Spanish explorer Ponce de León was the first European to visit Florida. He landed there in 1513, on the date of Spain's Easter festival of flowers. He also saw beautiful flowers growing in the new land. So he named the region Florida, a Spanish word meaning "full of flowers." (*See* **Ponce de León.**)

The Spanish built settlements and tried to convert the Indians to Christianity. In 1565, they built St. Augustine, the first town founded by Europeans in the present-day United States.

The United States claimed the western part of Florida in 1810. In 1821, Spain turned over the Florida peninsula to the United States. The next year, Florida became a U.S. territory.

48

GEORGIA

Tallahassee ★

St. Mary's River

Jacksonville

Arlington

FLORIDA

ATLANTIC OCEAN

Gulf of Mexico

River

Suwannee River

Gainesville

△ UNIVERSITY OF FLORIDA

St. Augustine
FIRST PERMANENT SETTLEMENT IN THE U.S.

▲ Historical Sites and Points of Interest

Ocala

St. Johns River

Daytona Beach

Witnlacoochee River

Sanford

Titusville

Winter Park

CAPE CANAVERAL

Orlando

Cocoa

Orange blossom

Tarpon Springs

Lakeland

Winter Haven

Tampa

Clearwater

Pinellas Park

St. Petersburg

Tampa Bay

Bradenton

Sarasota

WINTER CIRCUS QUARTERS

Peace River

Sebring

Fort Pierce

Mockingbird

Lake Okeechobee

West Palm Beach

Lake Worth

Fort Meyers

Boca Raton

Fort Lauderdale

SEMINOLE INDIAN RESERVATION △

Hollywood

North Miami

Miami Beach

Hialeah

Miami

Coral Gables

EVERGLADES NATIONAL PARK △

Key West

Florida Keys

Straits of Florida

Warm weather and sandy beaches make Florida a favorite vacation state.

The only Indians living in Florida in 1822 were the Seminoles. They fought a bitter war against the United States between 1835 and 1842, and were finally defeated. Most of them were sent to Indian reservations in the West, but a few hundred fled to the Everglades in southern Florida. Some of their descendants still live there.

On March 3, 1845, Florida became the 27th state of the United States. At the time of the Civil War, Florida joined the Confederate States of America and fought against the North. The state rejoined the Union in 1868.

Florida began gaining population during the late 1800s. Railroads were built out to its beaches. Then came hotels, and vacationers began to visit the state. Retired people settled in Florida because of its mild climate. More and more farms were started.

In the 1950s, the United States built a launching site at Cape Canaveral. Hundreds of rockets have been sent into space from the Kennedy Space Center at Cape Canaveral.

flour

Flour is a fine powder made by grinding grain. Most flour in the United States comes from wheat. Other grains—such as rye, corn, millet, and rice—are also ground into flour. Some flour is made from foods that are not grains. Potatoes, peanuts, and beans can all be ground into flour.

Flour is used for making bread, piecrust, pizza, cake, cookies, spaghetti and other kinds of pasta, pancakes, waffles, and tortillas. Flour is also used to thicken gravy, to coat meat and fish, and to make some sauces.

There are different kinds of wheat flour. The main kinds are *bread flour* and *cake flour*. Bread flour has *gluten,* which makes the bread chewy. Cake flour is low in gluten. This makes a cake tender and crumbly. There are different kinds of wheat. Flour from durum wheat is usually used in making pasta. Some flour sold in stores is *self-rising.* That means baking soda or baking powder, which makes a cake rise, has already been added to the flour.

Most wheat flour we use is white flour. Parts of the wheat grain—the bran and the germ—have been removed. Because these parts contain many vitamins and minerals, most flour is *enriched.* That means that vitamins and minerals have been added. Many white flours are also *bleached*—chemicals have been added to make them even whiter. Some people prefer unbleached flour. Another kind of flour is *whole-wheat flour.* Whole- wheat flour still has the bran and the germ. It is darker in color than white flour.

People have been making flour for more than 10,000 years. At first, people used stones to grind grain into flour. After a while, animals did the hard work, by turning huge millstones. Then windmills were used in some countries to turn the stones. People called *millers* ground the grain at their *mills.* Later steam power, water power, and electricity provided the energy for the mills. Now flour is usually made in large factories. This allows a great deal of flour to be produced.

See also **bread** and **grain.**

flower

Flowers are the parts of a plant we usually notice first. They are often brightly colored. They may have beautiful shapes and wonderful smells. But flowers are not just for people to enjoy. They do a very important job for plants. Flowers are the way flowering plants reproduce.

Flour can be made from grains, potatoes, or nuts. We use flour to make breads, pie crusts, cakes, and many other foods.

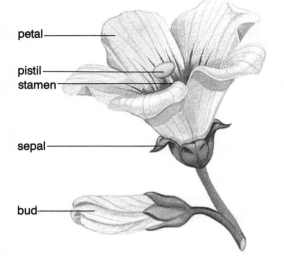

petal

pistil

stamen

sepal

bud

As a bud opens into a flower, you can see the flower parts inside.

Parts of a Flower A flower is made up of four kinds of parts: sepals, petals, stamens, and pistils. The first three kinds are arranged in circles.

The sepals form the outer circle. They are easiest to see before the flower bud opens. The sepals of most flowers are green, leaflike parts that cover and protect the bud. As the bud opens, the sepals fold back. They look like little leaves around the base of the flower. Some flowers, such as lilies, may have brightly colored sepals that look much like the petals of the flower.

The petals form the second circle. These are the brightly colored parts we picture when we think of flowers. Petals come in many different sizes, shapes, and colors. Rose petals may be red, pink, white, orange, or yellow. Violet petals are blue, purple, or white. Petals of some lilies have spots on them. Petals of gazania—a kind of daisy—are often striped. Poppy petals are separate from one another. You can pull out one petal at a time. Petunia petals are joined. The petunia looks like it has one large petal that goes all around. The petals of the balloonflower grow together, completely covering the inside of the flower. Each flower looks like a tiny blue or white balloon.

The next circle is made by the *stamens*. These structures look like little knobs at the end of stiff threads. Stamens are the male parts of the flower. The knobs are where *pollen* is produced.

At the center of the flower are the *pistils*. These are the female parts of the flower. Eggs are produced in the base of the pistil. Some kinds of flowers have only one pistil. Other kinds have many pistils joined together so closely that they look like just one.

Flower Forms Flowers are arranged in different ways on different kinds of plants. Roses may produce one or two flowers on a branch. A snapdragon shows off its flowers along a spike. The flowers begin opening at the bottom of the spike. Each day, more flowers open, until the spike is covered by flowers. Flowers of bleeding heart grow along one side of a branch. When they are open, they look like a row of tiny, pink hearts hanging from the branch. Other plants produce flowers in groups. What we call a geranium "flower" is really many small flowers, all in a bunch.

Sunflowers and daisies look like single large flowers. Colorful petals surround a central disk. But if you look closely, you see that each petal surrounding the disk is a separate flower. The disk itself is made up of dozens or even hundreds of tiny flowers. The petals of the disk flowers are so small that you might not recognize them as petals. When someone gives you a sunflower or a daisy, he or she is not giving you a single flower. You are receiving a whole bouquet!

We think of a daisy as one flower, but its center is really dozens of tiny flowers.

Many flowers have sepals, petals, stamens, and pistils, but many others do not have all four parts. Grasses—one of the largest groups of flowering plants—have very small flowers. Grass flowers have stamens and pistils that are covered by a leaflike structure called a *bract*. But they do not have petals and sepals.

Female and Male Flowers Some kinds of plants produce two kinds of flowers. Some of the flowers contain stamens and are male flowers. Some of the flowers contain pistils and are female flowers. In cucumber, squash, and watermelon plants, both kinds of flowers are on the same plant. If you have ever grown these plants, you may have noticed that only some of the flowers produce fruit. The flowers that grow into fruits are female flowers. The male flowers produce pollen and then die.

Holly trees are another flowering plant that produces two kinds of flowers. But the male flowers and female flowers are not on the same tree. They are on two separate trees. The red berries only form on the tree that has female flowers.

Pollination For most flowering plants to reproduce, pollen has to be carried from the stamens of one flower to the pistils of another flower of the same kind. Moving pollen from one flower to another, or from one plant to another, is called *pollination*. Usually, flowers are pollinated by animals, or by the wind. But people sometimes pollinate flowers in order to produce plants with particular qualities. (*See* **pollination**.)

The structure of a flower tells a lot about how it is pollinated. Flowers with large, showy petals are usually pollinated by birds or insects. A few flowers are pollinated by bats or rodents. The colors and shapes of the petals attract the animals to the flowers. The smell of a flower also attracts them.

Animals do not visit flowers with pollination in mind. They come to eat. Hummingbirds and many insects feed on the sweet juice of many flowers. This juice is called *nectar*. Other insects feed on the flower's pollen. As these animals feed, some of the pollen clings to their legs and bodies. When the animal goes to another flower, some of the pollen goes along, too.

These female flowers will grow into squashes—baby squashes are already developing on the stem. Male flowers produce pollen but do not develop into fruit.

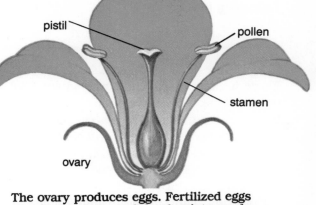

The ovary produces eggs. Fertilized eggs stay in the ovary and develop into seeds.

Brightly colored flowers usually attract hummingbirds, bees, and butterflies. White flowers attract moths at night. The moths are dusted with pollen as they feed. They carry this pollen to other plants.

Many grasses and trees have small flowers without petals. These flowers are pollinated by the wind. Flowers pollinated by the wind produce a great amount of pollen. When the pollen is ripe, even a gentle breeze can pick it up and carry it to other plants. If you suffer from hay fever, you know when grasses are producing pollen. The pollen in the air makes some people sneeze and have watery eyes. (*See* **allergy**.)

Pollen is made up of microscopic pollen grains. When seen under a microscope, pollen grains have a beautiful structure. Some are covered by ridges and valleys. Others have tiny spikes sticking out of them. The pollen of each kind of flowering plant has a specific shape. Biologists who study pollen can often identify plants just by looking at the pollen grains.

Microscopic grains of pollen (right) look like a dusting of powder on the flower.

Seed Production When pollen grains land on the pistil of a flower, pollination is completed. Now the pollen grains begin to swell. A tiny tube grows from each pollen grain. As the tube grows, it burrows down into the pistil. Eventually, the tube grows into the ovary, at the base of the pistil. Materials from the pollen tube join with the eggs in the ovary and fertilize them.

After the eggs are fertilized, changes begin to appear in the flower. Often its petals wither and fall off. The fertilized eggs inside the ovary grow into seeds. Each seed contains a tiny new plant and a supply of food. The strong outer covering of the seed protects the new plant.

The growing ovary develops into a fruit, which forms around the seed or seeds. Apples, grapes, cherries, and oranges are fruits. To scientists, tomatoes, squashes, beans, peppers, and peas are also fruits, even though we think of them as vegetables. Some things we think of as nuts—acorns, walnuts, and pecans—are fruits, too. All of these things are fertilized in the same way.

We enjoy the beauty of flowers. We grow them in our yards, or buy them from a florist, and arrange them in bouquets. We use them for happy times, such as weddings, and for sad times, such as funerals. We make perfumes from their scents. We depend on them for food. When we eat broccoli, we are eating flower buds. When we eat bread and pasta, we are eating food made from the seeds of flowers.

See also **flowering plant; fruit; plant;** and **plant breeding.**

flowering plant

Flowering plants are found everywhere. Like other plants, they have roots, stems, and leaves. But unlike other plants, they have flowers. Some flowers come in beautiful colors and shapes. They also smell lovely. But a flower's real purpose is to make seeds so the plant can reproduce.

Flowering plants come in many different forms. Daisies, African violets, cherry trees, rosebushes, and sweet potatoes are only a few of the world's flowering plants. Some, like duckweed plants, are tiny. Others, like oak trees, are huge.

Some have soft stems and leaves and live for only one growing season. They are called *annuals*. Many garden plants—such as snapdragons, petunias, spinach, and beans —are annuals. Others have woody stems or can store food in their roots. These can live for many years and are called *perennials*. Rosebushes, grasses, and flowering trees are some of the common perennials.

There are also *biennials*—plants that live for two years. During the first year, these plants usually store food. In the second year, they flower and die. People eat many biennial vegetables. Carrots, beets, cabbages, and onions are biennials. Because people eat them before the plants flower, you may never have seen their flowers.

hibiscus

rhododendron

forsythia

annuals

perennials

celosia

marigold

flowering grasses

iris

biennials

petunia

impatiens

pansy

onion

cabbage

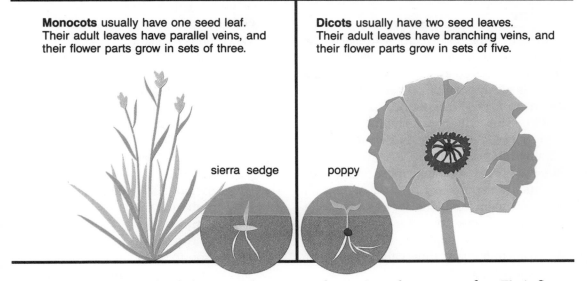

Monocots usually have one seed leaf. Their adult leaves have parallel veins, and their flower parts grow in sets of three.

sierra sedge

Dicots usually have two seed leaves. Their adult leaves have branching veins, and their flower parts grow in sets of five.

poppy

Flowering plants are divided into two large groups. Grasses, onions, and lilies belong to one group. Their leaves are long and narrow, like straps. The petals or other parts of their flowers are in groups of three. When their seeds sprout, each sprout has only one *seed leaf.* Seed leaves are the first leaves that show on a young plant. Plants with only one seed leaf are called *monocots.*

The second group of flowering plants includes dandelions, apple trees, pussy willows, and garden peas. Their leaves come in many shapes—oval, round, hand-shaped, and star-shaped, to name a few. Their flower parts are in groups of four or five. When the seeds sprout, they send up two seed leaves. These plants are called *dicots.*

Many flowering plants produce bright, showy blossoms. Poppies, tulips, and magnolia trees are just three examples. But many other flowering plants have small, dull-colored flowers. In fact, you may never notice their flowers at all. Grasses and many trees have flowers that are hard to see, but they are still flowering plants. (*See* **grasses.**)

See also **flower** and **plant.**

The African violet is a flowering plant that grows well indoors.

day lily

hosta

sweet william

foxglove

forget-me-not

carrot

fluorine

By itself, fluorine (FLU-reen) is a pale-yellow gas that is poisonous and strong-smelling. But fluorine never appears by itself in nature. It is always combined with some other element to form a compound, called a *fluoride.* Fluorine will even combine with the "noble gases," elements that do not react with anything else.

We use fluorides to make most refrigerator coolants, nonstick coatings for pots and pans, and foam cushions for car seats. We also add fluorides to water supplies and toothpastes. Tiny amounts of these fluorides, used over a long time, can help prevent cavities in people's teeth.

Even though fluorine is poisonous by itself, almost all the fluorides are nonpoisonous. One major exception is hydrogen fluoride, a powerful acid that will even eat holes in glass containers!

fly

A fly is a kind of insect. The most common fly is the housefly. It lives wherever people live. Other well-known flies include horseflies, fruit flies, botflies, mosquitoes, and tsetse flies.

Flies have six legs and two wings. The wings may vibrate 200 to 1,000 times every second. That is what causes the buzzing

sound we hear. Flies also have sticky pads on their feet. That is why they can walk upside down on ceilings!

Most flies feed on liquids. The mouthparts of a fly form a tube. They use their tubes to pierce the skin of animals or plants and suck up blood or plant juices.

A fly's life has four stages: egg, larva, pupa, and adult. The larvae, which hatch from the eggs, look like little worms. They are called *maggots.* When the larvae are fully grown, they enter the pupa stage. While in the pupa stage, they change into adults. Only the adults have wings.

Many flies are serious pests. Some flies, including mosquitoes, can transmit diseases. The larvae of many flies also feed on farm crops.

Other flies are helpful to people. Some pollinate plants or eat harmful insects or decaying waste materials.

See also **insect** and **mosquitoes and gnats.**

fog

Fog is a cloud that is close to the ground. Like all clouds, it is made up of tiny drops of water. If the temperature is below freezing, the fog may be made up of ice crystals. (*See* **cloud.**)

You can see a small amount of fog forming near the spout of a teakettle when the water in the kettle is boiling. Inside the teakettle, water turns into invisible *water vapor*—the gas phase of water. As the water vapor

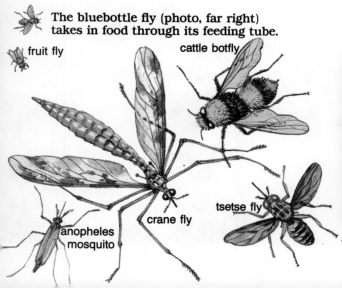

The bluebottle fly (photo, far right) takes in food through its feeding tube.

fruit fly

cattle botfly

crane fly

anopheles mosquito

tsetse fly

bluebottle fly

housefly

Ground fog settles in valleys. When the sun comes out, the fog disappears. A steam iron (right) sprays foglike water vapor.

rushes out of the spout, some of it is cooled by the air around it. It begins to turn into tiny drops of liquid water and becomes visible as little puffs of fog. Although we call these little puffs "steam," they are more like fog. They are made of tiny drops of liquid water in the air.

Outdoors, fog forms when moist air is cooling. Nearly all air contains some invisible water vapor. Warm air can hold more water vapor than cool air. As air cools, it finally reaches a temperature where it cannot hold all of its water vapor. This temperature is called the air's *dew point.* When the air's temperature goes below the dew point, some of the invisible water vapor changes into tiny drops of liquid water. The colder the air becomes, the more drops form. (*See* **dew.**)

At first, these tiny drops form a light fog called a *mist.* If the air continues to cool, the fog may become so thick that people can see only a few yards in any direction.

Fog forms easily along ocean shores. Warm, moist air from over the ocean settles over colder land. As the moist air cools, fog begins to form. Sometimes, fog seems to "roll in" from over the ocean. Fog can also form over land when a warm, moist air mass meets a cool, dry air mass.

Some places are famous for their fogs. Warm, moist air often blows from the Pacific Ocean over northern California and forms fog. In Ireland and Great Britain, warm ocean air often settles over colder land and creates thick fog. San Francisco, California, and London, England, are two cities famous for their fogs.

Fog also forms on clear, cloudless nights in valleys and hollows near lakes and rivers. On a clear night, the earth can cool quickly. Moist air from over a lake or river settles into a valley. It soon cools past its dew point, and the valley fills with fog.

Fog is a special danger to sailors and pilots. At sea, a ship may sometimes be in a fog for days at a time. Sailors cannot see lighthouses or lighted buoys during a fog. They may have to listen for foghorns, which warn of dangerous rocks. Large modern ships may have radar, which can find rocks and other objects through the thickest fog. Pilots can use radar to find their way in dense fog.

Fog may disappear in two ways. If moist, foggy air cools very quickly, the tiny drops of water in the fog join together to form raindrops. The fog will then clear up as it begins to rain.

The second way fog disappears is through warming. When the sun comes up in the morning, it warms the air in the valleys and hollows. The tiny drops of water in the air turn back into water vapor, which is invisible. The fog just seems to vanish.

See also **weather.**

folk dance

People have always danced. Over the years, groups of people have developed their own dances. These traditional dances are folk dances.

Some folk dances celebrate happy events, such as a marriage or the birth of a child. Others mourn the death of a person or mark some other unhappy event.

Some folk dances are courtship dances. In these, a man dances as a way of asking a woman to marry him. The Mexican hat dance is a courtship dance.

Folk dances may be part of religious worship. Some dances were once parts of religious events, but their religious meaning has been forgotten. For example, in many countries, people dance around a Maypole on May Day. Long ago, Maypole dances were probably part of a religious ceremony asking the gods to help the crops grow. Today, people dance them for fun.

People once thought some folk dances could help them control mysterious forces such as death, disease, or the weather. The tarantella, a popular Italian folk dance, began as a way of curing the bite of a tarantula, a poisonous spider. American Indian rain dances were used to bring rain.

Today, people dance mostly to have fun. Every country has its own popular folk dances. In the United States, for example, square dancing is popular. American square dances are a little different from dances in other parts of the world.

In colonial America, playing music and dancing was considered sinful. So people made up "games" that were like dances, but were not considered sinful. Today, we still sing the songs for some of these game-dances—"Skip to My Lou," "Shoo Fly," and "The Bluetail Fly" (also known as "Jimmie Crack Corn").

There are four important kinds of folk dances. The oldest is the circle dance. All the dancers dance in a circle. The Jewish *Hora* and the Greek *Syrto* are circle dances.

A second kind is the square dance. Usually, eight dancers form a square, two to each side. In some square dances, a "caller" shouts instructions to the dancers.

Yugoslavian folk dancers in traditional dress do an ancient circle dance.

A third kind is the contra dance. The dancers form two lines facing each other. The Virginia reel is a contra dance.

In the fourth kind of folk dance, people dance in couples. Usually, a man and a woman dance together. These dances are often courtship dances.

See also **folk song.**

folk song

Folk songs are the traditional songs of a community. Everyone in the community knows them. New songs may become popular for a while and then fade away. But folk songs remain favorites. People may sing them together when they are working, celebrating, or playing.

Often, no one knows who first wrote the tune or the words for a folk song. Sometime in the past, someone made up the song. Other people liked it and began to sing it, too. Soon, all the people in the community knew it. They sang it to their children. Their children grew up and sang it to their own children. The song was passed down from parent to child through the years.

Some folk songs are work songs. People often sang them as they worked. It made the work seem easier and lifted their spirits. Black slaves in the United States had many work songs, such as "Pick a Bale of Cotton." Sailors sang "Blow the Man Down" and many others. Cowboys had lots of songs. "Get Along Little Dogie" and "Home on the Range" are just two of them. Men laying down railroad tracks sang "Casey Jones" and "I've Been Working on the Railroad."

Many folk songs are about things that changed people's lives, or things that made them very sad or very happy. Some songs tell about great heroes. "John Henry" is about a great railroad worker who had a contest with a machine. "John Brown's Body" is about a man who died fighting against slavery.

There are also folk songs about war. "When Johnny Comes Marching Home Again" was a song of the U.S. Civil War.

This man makes folk-music instruments like the mountain dulcimer at bottom.

Many folk songs are about love, marriage, and family life. There are also many religious folk songs, including *spirituals*—such as "Swing Low, Sweet Chariot"—and Christmas *carols*—such as "The First Noel."

Funny folk songs make people laugh. "Froggie Went A-Courtin'" is about a frog who marries a mouse. Sometimes folk songs are used in playing games or while doing folk dances. Two very old folk songs of this kind are "Ring-Around-the-Rosy" and "London Bridge."

American folk songs became especially popular in the 1930s, when many people first got radios and record players. Some folk singers became stars. They sang in big concerts and recorded their songs. Woody Guthrie sang old folk songs, but also sang new songs about the poor. Today, many folk singers sing about peace, ending world hunger, and other important issues.

See also **music** and **folk dance.**

food

Food is what we eat. Food is a basic need of all living things. It supplies the nutrients we need for growth and repair. It gives energy for all the body's activities.

Green plants make their food from sunlight and the chemicals inside them. Other living creatures cannot make their own food. They either eat plants, or they eat animals that eat plants. (*See* **food chain.**)

Some living things eat only one kind of food. Giant pandas, for example, eat mainly bamboo shoots. When bamboo shoots are scarce, many giant pandas die. Other animals can eat a variety of foods. Human beings probably eat the widest variety of foods. Because of this, human beings can live almost anyplace on earth. Living things that can eat a variety of foods have a better chance of surviving.

How People Get Food Thousands of years ago, people spent most of their time gathering food. People searched for food and ate whatever they found. They ate wild plants and perhaps some small insects. They learned what was safe to eat. They learned to catch fish and to trap small animals.

When we go fishing or pick berries, we are hunting and gathering as humans did in prehistoric times.

After a while, people organized groups to hunt large animals. A large animal could feed many people. To hunt better, people invented tools such as spears and bows and arrows. By this time, people had learned to use fire and to cook some of their food. They learned to dry food and store it, so it would keep without spoiling.

Two new ways of life began when people started to raise their own animals and to plant their own food. One way of life was herding. The herders were *nomads*. With their flocks of sheep, goats, or cattle, they wandered in search of food for their animals. The nomads used their animals' milk and meat for food. They also gathered plant foods. (*See* **nomad.**)

The other way of life was farming. People settled in an area and planted grains and other crops. Their crops gave them a regular supply of food. Many farmers also raised animals, for milk and for food.

After a while, farmers were producing enough food to feed many people. Now everyone did not have to raise food. Some people could spend their time making pottery, metal goods, cloth, and other goods. They could trade their products for food.

New tools and farming methods helped farmers grow more food. The plow was invented, and farmers began using animals to do the heavy work. Farmers in many parts of the world learned to *irrigate* their fields to bring in water. A steady water supply meant better crops.

In the 1700s and 1800s, farmers began using scientific methods to raise better plants and animals. People learned that if they planted a different crop each season, the field would stay fertile. They learned to breed animals so that each new generation supplied more meat. New farm machines sped up planting and harvesting. In the 1900s, farmers used chemical fertilizers to increase the amount of food an acre of land could produce. They also bred plants that could resist disease. (*See* **farming; fertilizer; and plant breeding.**)

Until the 1800s, foods had to be preserved by drying, smoking, pickling, or making jams or jellies (left). Today we can freeze or refrigerate foods or buy them in cans and vacuum packs.

Some less-developed countries still do not grow enough food. Their farmers use very old tools and methods. Some countries are improving their methods so they can produce more food.

Keeping Food In colder climates, fruits, vegetables, and nuts grow only in spring and summer. To have enough to eat in the winter, people learned to preserve and store food. Some animals and insects also store food for the winter.

People found different ways of preserving food. Fruits, vegetables, and berries could be dried. Milk was made into cheese, which lasted longer than fresh milk. Meat and fish were smoked or salted. Some foods were kept covered with sugar and spices. Grains, roots, and beans lasted a long time when kept dry. People also found that foods lasted longer if kept cold. People had no refrigerators, so they packed food in snow or ice.

In the last 200 years, other ways to keep food were invented. People began sealing food in sterile jars in 1795. In the early 1800s, food went into metal cans. Today, refrigerators keep food cold in homes and restaurants. Refrigerated trains, trucks, ships, and airplanes make it possible to ship foods over long distances. People who live far from water can get fresh fish, and people who live in cold climates can get fresh fruit from warm climates in winter.

Freezing is another important way to preserve vegetables, fruits, meats, and other foods. There are also new forms of sterile packaging in paper containers. Juices and milk in these containers can last several months without refrigeration. Some food is *irradiated*—x-rayed—to kill harmful bacteria. (*See* **food processing**.)

Food in Different Places The preservation and transportation of food has made a variety of foods available any time of the year. But in most parts of the world, people still eat mainly the foods that grow in their regions. People who live near the sea eat a lot of fish. In South America, where corn grows well, people use corn in different ways every day. Wheat grows in North America and most of Europe. People in these places eat lots of wheat cereals, wheat breads, and other wheat products. Rice is part of almost every meal in Asia, South America, and Greece.

Food and Customs For most peoples of the world, eating is more than just a way to stay alive. Foods and eating have taken on special meanings. Families and friends eat meals together. Foods are offered to guests to make them feel welcome. Foods are part of holiday celebrations, such as Thanksgiving dinner in the United States. Many religions have rules about what foods a person can eat and how the foods should be prepared. Certain foods are also included in religious ceremonies. At the *seder*—a special meal eaten at Passover—Jews eat certain foods in a certain order as a way of giving thanks to God.

See also **nutrition; cooking;** and **eating customs.**

People share special food—such as ice cream—to celebrate a happy occasion.

Corn provides flour for corn breads and breakfast foods, corn oil for cooking, corn syrup for sweetening, and cornstarch for thickening. It also provides popcorn!

FOOD NAMES

We can tell something about where our foods came from by where we got their names.

From American Indian languages

barbecue	Taino *barbacoa* (a frame of sticks for roasting meat)
chocolate	Aztec *chocolatl*
hominy	Algonquian *rockahominie*
potato	Taino *batata*
squash	Narragansett *asquatasquash*
tomato	Aztec *tomatl*

From languages of Europe

bagel	Yiddish *beygel* (round loaf)
cafeteria	Spanish (coffee house)
chowder	French *chaudière* (kettle)
coleslaw	Dutch *koolsla* (cabbage salad)
cookie	Dutch *koekje* (little cake)
croissant	French (crescent)
frankfurter	German city named Frankfurt, where sausage was invented
hamburger	German city named Hamburg, where it was invented
lasagna	Italian (cooking pot)
lox	Yiddish *laks* (salmon)
spaghetti	Italian (little strings)
waffle	Dutch *wafel* (wafer)

From other parts of the world

chow	Chinese *ch'ao* (to cook)
orange	Arabic *naranj*
yam	Sengalese *nyami*

food chain

Every living thing needs food. Plants can make their own food from sunlight and water. Animals cannot make their own food, so they must eat plants or other living things.

At the same time, every living thing becomes food for some other living thing. For example, grass grows in a meadow. Rabbits eat grass. Hawks eat baby rabbits. We call a list like this a *food chain*. Food chains help biologists understand how plants and animals live. Biologists use arrows to show what gets eaten by what.

grass ⟶ rabbit ⟶ hawk

There are thousands of different food chains. The one above is a food chain in a meadow. A food chain in African grasslands starts with grass, too, but after that, this food chain is very different.

grass ⟶ antelope ⟶ lion

There are food chains not only on land but in air and water, too. For example, this food chain tells about living things in a cold lake or stream.

algae ⟶ insect larvae ⟶ trout

Insect larvae eat algae that grow in the water. Many of the larvae become food for fish such as trout.

In this food chain, a grasshopper eats a plant, a frog eats the grasshopper, a snake eats the frog, and a hawk eats the snake.

Producers and Consumers Almost all food chains begin with some kind of plant. Plants are called *producers* because they produce their own food from sunlight and water.

All other living things in a food chain are *consumers*. Since they cannot make their own food as plants do, they must *consume*—eat—one or more kinds of plant or animal material. The smallest insect and the largest whale are consumers. So are many tiny organisms, such as fungi and bacteria.

Consumers that eat plant parts are the second link in a food chain. They are sometimes called *herbivores,* which means "plant-eaters." Insect larvae eat leaves. Bees take liquid nectar from flowers. Many digging animals, such as voles and gophers, eat roots. Termites eat wood. Cows, sheep, horses, and some other large consumers are *grazers.* They eat grains and grasses.

Consumers that eat other animals are called *carnivores,* a word meaning "meat-eaters." Lions, eagles, snakes, spiders, and frogs are some of the carnivores. You probably can name many others.

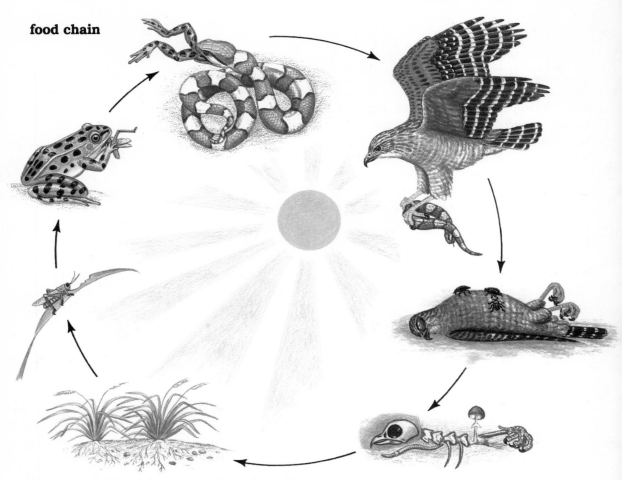

food chain

A food chain is really a circle. When the hawk dies, tiny creatures in the soil decompose its body. A plant uses the decomposed material for nourishment. Then one day, a grasshopper eats the plant, and the chain begins again.

Some carnivores are *predators*. They hunt and kill other animals for food. Others are *scavengers*, eating the remains of what other animals have killed, or animals that have died of natural causes. In Africa, hyenas and jackals often follow lions. They eat the leftovers after the lion has fed. In the western United States, the magpie is a common scavenger. Vultures are scavengers that live all over the world. They eat the remains of dead animals.

Consumers that eat both plants and animals are called *omnivores*. Humans are omnivores. So are bears, raccoons, turtles, and monkeys.

Decomposers One special kind of consumer is called a *decomposer*. Decomposers break down the dead bodies of all living things. For this reason, they are often called "nature's garbage collectors."

Fungi and bacteria are important decomposers in almost all food chains. If you cut grass, decomposers will cause the grass clippings to "rot" and slowly disappear. When an animal dies in the wild, many different living things may feed on it. Scavengers may eat part of it. Insects may come and lay eggs so their larvae can eat part. Finally, tiny decomposers finish the work. Nothing is left except, perhaps, the animal's bones. And even the bones may disappear after a while.

Decomposers are very important because they "close" the circle of the food chain. They break down dead things into substances that plants use to make food. They send a gas called *carbon dioxide* into the air. They also make other chemicals that seep into the soil. Plants use sunlight and these chemicals to produce new food. They start the food chain all over again.

Food Webs An animal may eat more than one thing. It may also become food for more than one other creature. So most food chains are connected with many other food chains. We call this a *food web.* The diagram below shows how complicated a food web can become.

Squirrels, blue jays, and mice all eat nuts. A baby squirrel may become food for an owl. A grown squirrel, a rabbit, a blue jay, a frog, or a mouse may become food for a fox. A mouse can also be food for a cat, an owl, or a hawk. And all around there are decomposers, the tiny creatures that will help break down the remains of old buried nuts, other plant matter, and dead animals.

This food web shows only a few of the food chains that may exist in one small area. A complete food web might include 50 or more living things.

See also **biome; ecology; environment;** and **food.**

Many living things eat more than one kind of food. For this reason, food chains can fit together to make a complex food web.

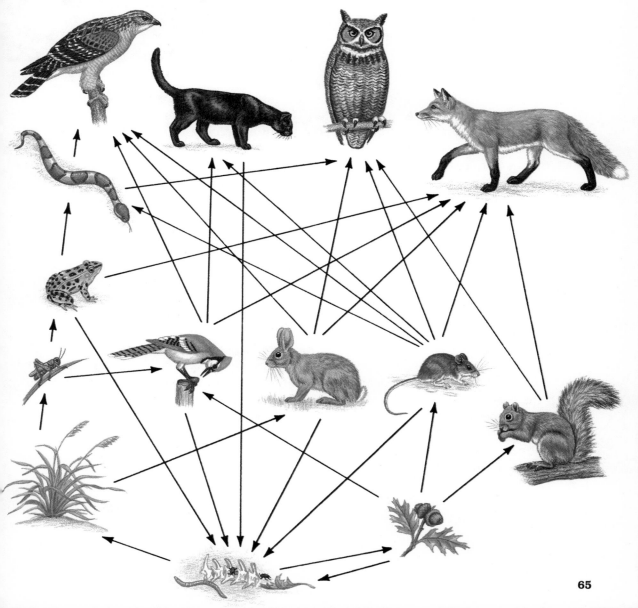

food processing

Unless you eat only fresh, uncooked meat and vegetables, and drink milk straight from the cow, your diet includes mainly processed foods. Anything that is done to a food, even mashing peanuts into peanut butter or boiling an egg, is a kind of food processing.

Boiling eggs is a simple kind of food processing.

Our most basic foods are processed. Wheat, for example, is the seed of a grass. It cannot be digested by humans unless it is processed. First, the grain—seed—is separated from its hard coatings. Then the grain is ground into flour. Flour is mixed with other ingredients and then baked to make bread, or dried to make pasta. All these steps are needed to make the wheat digestible for people.

Food is processed for many reasons. Processing makes food easier to prepare, eat, and digest. Processing also allows us to add vitamins and minerals or flavors and colors. But the oldest and most important reason for processing food is to preserve it—to keep it from spoiling. Preserving foods allows us to eat a variety of foods all year long, not just during the growing season. It also enables us to export foods to countries where there is not enough food.

Food Preservation Until the late 1800s, when Louis Pasteur studied microscopic bacteria, no one really knew what caused food to spoil. Pasteur realized that bacteria are everywhere—in air, soil, and water. This means they are in our bodies and in our food. He showed that the bacteria caused food to spoil.

Tomatoes being washed at a canning plant.

Early humans had already found ways to keep food from spoiling. They knew nothing about bacteria, but they discovered that drying food made it last longer. A fresh grape spoils quickly. A dried grape—a raisin—can be kept much longer. Bacteria, like all living things, need water. By removing water from foods, our ancestors made it more difficult for bacteria to survive.

Early humans also found that meat dried faster if they covered it with salt. The salt absorbed much of the moisture. Dried meat is tough and salty, but it remains free of mold much longer than raw, unsalted meat.

By the early 1800s, people were preserving foods in glass jars and tin-plated steel cans. Many people today still cook and can their own fruit and vegetables. Jarring and canning require great care. The containers, lids, and foods must be heated to kill all bacteria. Each container must be tightly sealed to keep bacteria from getting in later.

Chemicals and Food People have long used *brine*—salt water—for preserving and flavoring foods. If you buy a jar of pickles, you will find that they are in brine or vinegar. Cucumbers last longer as pickles.

After discovering that brine and vinegar preserved food, people began experimenting

In a food-processing plant, a worker uses a machine that puts frosting on rolls.

with other chemicals to preserve food. If you read the labels on food packages, you will see names and initials of chemicals that are used today to keep the food fresh.

Ingredients on labels are listed in order of amount. These are the ingredients in a chocolate cupcake with cream filling:

Sugar, water, enriched flour (contains niacin, iron, thiamine mononitrate, riboflavin), vegetable and/or animal shortening, corn syrup, skim milk, cocoa, whey, starch, leavening, salt, chocolate liquor, mono/glycerides and diglycerides, gelatin, sodium phosphate, agar, lecithin, natural and artificial flavors, artificial colors, sorbic acid.

Chemicals are also used for other kinds of food processing. Dyes give such foods as margarine and bacon a more appealing color. Gums give foods a better texture. Other chemicals are used to change the flavor of foods.

Fire and Cold Learning to make and use fire led to new ways of processing and preserving food. Fire made it possible for people to process rice and wheat into a variety of foods. There was no popcorn, no bread, no sugar, until people learned to cook with fire.

High temperatures killed most bacteria. Smoking killed even more bacteria. It also coated the food with a thin layer of smoke particles that kept out bacteria from the air. Many people today enjoy smoked bacon, beef, fish, and cheeses.

People who lived in cold climates soon found that freezing food kept it fresh. But until the early 1900s, when refrigerators and freezers were invented, ice was very difficult for most people to get—and to keep. Since the 1950s, people have been able to buy frozen foods.

Freeze-drying was developed during World War II. Today, it is an important food process. "Instant" soups, coffee, seasoning mixes, juices, and many more foods are freeze-dried. Their water is removed, and they are sealed in airtight packages.

Many people avoid heavily processed foods. Medical experts discovered that some chemical preservatives were dangerous. Laws were passed against using these harmful chemicals in food. But if people had not developed ways to process food, we would probably be spending almost all our time searching for food, as the first humans did.

See also **cooking** and **refrigeration.**

football

Every weekend in the fall, thousands of football teams play football. They play on fields and in stadiums across the United States and Canada. Many young players dream of becoming football stars.

Football is also a popular sport to watch. Professional teams usually play on Sunday afternoons. Millions of fans watch the games on television. College and university teams play on Saturdays. Many high schools play on Fridays.

How Football Is Played Football has many rules, but the idea of the game is simple. Two teams, of 11 players each, play on a large, flat field. One team wants to get the football and move it over the goal line at one end of the field. The other team wants to move the ball across the goal line at the other end of the field. The team without the ball tries to stop the team that has the ball. They do this by *tackling*—knocking down—the player who is holding the ball.

A football is shaped something like an egg, but its ends are more pointed. Since football can be very rough, players wear hard helmets, shoulder pads, and other padding to protect them.

A football field is 120 yards long. The goal lines are 10 yards from each end. That leaves 100 yards between the two goals. The field is marked with a white line every five yards.

A football game begins with a *kickoff*. A player on one team kicks the ball down the field to the other team. The player who catches it runs toward his goal until he is tackled or until he runs out of bounds.

After the kickoff, the team with the ball has four plays, called *downs,* to move the ball 10 yards closer to their goal. If the players gain 10 yards, they get four more downs to move the ball another 10 yards. In this way, they try to work their way down the field to their goal.

A play starts with the ball set on the ground. The two teams line up facing each other. The center, a player on the team that

The team with the ball (left) tries to move it across the goal (right) for a score. At far right, a referee makes the signal for a score.

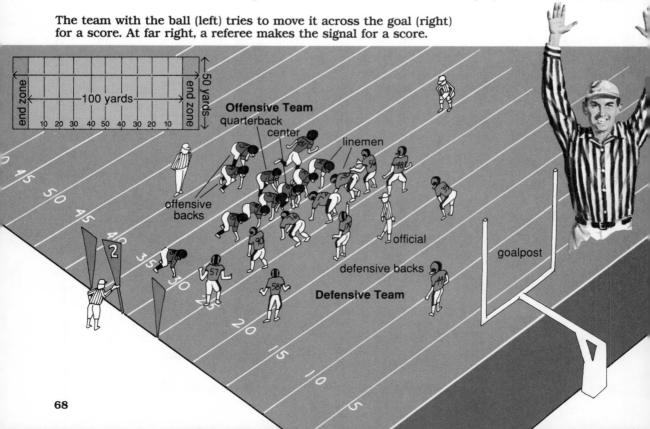

end zone | 100 yards | end zone | 50 yards
10 20 30 40 50 40 30 20 10

Offensive Team
quarterback
center
linemen
offensive backs
official
defensive backs
Defensive Team
goalpost

has the ball, hands or passes the ball between his legs to a teammate behind
him—usually the quarterback.

When the quarterback gets the ball, he can
move it forward in one of three ways. He can
run with the ball. He can hand off the ball to
another runner. Or he can *pass*—throw the
ball to a teammate. His other teammates try
to keep tacklers away from the ballcarrier. A
play ends when the player with the ball is
tackled or runs out of bounds, or when a
pass is not caught.

If a team can't move the ball 10 yards in
four downs, the other team gets the ball and
tries to move the ball toward their goal.

Scoring There are four ways to score in
football. If a team moves the ball across the
goal line with a run or a pass, they score a
touchdown, worth six points. The team scoring a touchdown also gets to try for an extra
point—a *point-after-touchdown.* Usually, a
player tries to score the point by kicking the
football between the *goalposts*—two upright
posts near the goal.

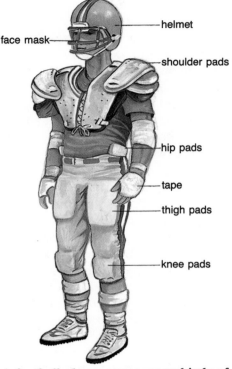

A football player wears many kinds of
padding to protect him from injury.

When a play starts, each player knows his job. When the quarterback gets the ball,
he may throw a pass, run with the ball himself, or hand it off to another runner.

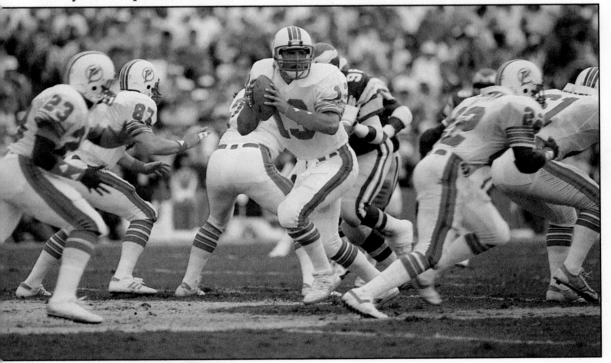

Sometimes, a team may decide that they won't be able to score a touchdown. Instead, the team may try to score a *field goal* by having a player kick the football between the goalposts from out in the field. A field goal is worth three points.

The fourth kind of score is called a *safety*. If the team without the ball can push the team with the ball back across the wrong goal, they score two points.

History People have played goal games for hundreds of years. In England in the 1200s, people played a kind of football on feast days. The field was the land between two villages. The teams were the people of the two villages. The ball was the leathery bladder of a pig or other animal, blown up like a balloon. Each team tried to kick the ball all the way to the other village. These games were so dangerous that people were often killed.

In the 1800s, students at boys' schools in England played a game something like soccer. Players tried to kick the ball down the field to the goal. Then in 1823, a boy at Rugby School picked up the ball and ran with it. This was against the rules, but many players liked the idea. So they made a new game called *rugby football.*

Boys in the United States began playing football in the 1860s. They, too, liked the idea of running with the ball, so they used some of the rugby rules. They also made up rules of their own. Soon, American football was quite different from the football played in other countries.

After 1900, college football became very popular. In the 1920s, players such as Jim Thorpe and Red Grange became national heroes. Towns in Pennsylvania and Ohio started the first professional teams.

In the 1950s and 1960s, television brought football into everyone's home. Soon it was one of the most popular spectator sports in the United States. Today, the Super Bowl—the championship game for professional teams—is watched by more people than any other sports event.

Gerald Ford was the only president who was not elected as president or vice president.

Ford, Gerald R.

Gerald Rudolph Ford was the 38th President of the United States. He served from 1974 to 1977.

Ford was born in 1913 in Omaha, Nebraska, but grew up in Grand Rapids, Michigan. He was the star center of his high school's football team. His football success continued at the University of Michigan. He coached football at Yale University, where he later went to law school.

Just as his law career was beginning, World War II interrupted it. Ford joined the U.S. Navy and served as an officer in the South Pacific.

Following the war, Ford grew interested in politics. In 1948, voters around Grand Rapids elected him to the House of Representatives. They reelected him every two years until Ford had served nearly 26 years. Republican congress members elected him their leader.

In 1973, the vice president of the United States, Spiro T. Agnew, resigned. President Richard M. Nixon appointed Gerald Ford vice president. Then, only a year later, Nixon resigned, and Ford became president. Ford became the first person in U.S. history to serve as president without being elected president *or* vice president.

Ford ran for president in 1976, but lost to Jimmy Carter. He left Washington and retired to Palm Springs, California.

Ford, Henry

Henry Ford did more than anyone else to make the automobile a part of life in the United States. He built cars that many people could afford.

Henry Ford was born in 1863, near Dearborn, Michigan. He grew up during an exciting time of new inventions. When he was a young man, the telegraph was making it possible to send messages quickly across huge distances. The telephone was being tried out. People had just begun to light their homes with electricity.

When he was 21, Ford's father gave him some farmland. Young Henry moved to the farm, but did not become a farmer. He preferred working with machines. After a few years, he took a job as a machinist.

Ford became interested in the internal-combustion engine—a kind of engine that could power an automobile. He experimented with engines in his spare time. By 1896, he had built his own car—the Quadracycle. It was the only car in Detroit. Ford sold his Quadracycle for $200. He used the money to build his next car. Soon the mayor of Detroit presented him with the city's very first driver's license.

Ford joined a new automobile company as chief engineer. But he soon left the company so he could build and drive his own racing cars. One of his cars, the Ford 999, won every race it entered. Racing made Henry Ford famous. Soon he was ready to set up his own company to make cars for sale.

In 1903, the year the Wright brothers flew their first airplane, Henry Ford formed the Ford Motor Company. He built cars that were reliable, simple to repair, and inexpensive. After trying several designs, Ford designed a car he called the Model T. The first

Henry Ford (left) used the assembly line (below) to make cars quickly and cheaply. Workers are sliding the car body down onto the frame. The engine and tires are already in place.

Model T was built in 1908. A year later, Ford announced that he would make nothing but Model Ts. The car became so popular that for several years Ford sold more cars than all other auto makers together. By 1927, more than 15 million had been sold.

Ford's method of making cars was the main reason for his success. In those days, most cars were built one at a time by a few master mechanics. In Ford's factory, cars moved along a *production line,* on a slow-moving belt. Each worker did just one job as each car moved by. Workers at the beginning of the production line put together the frame of each car. Workers farther down the line attached other parts. By the time a car reached the end of the production line, it was finished.

By using a production line, Ford could make cars quickly and cheaply. Workers became very fast, because they made the same movements over and over. Ford was able to charge less for his cars than other car builders could. He sold so many cars that he was able to pay his workers higher wages. To attract workers to his factories, Ford paid them $5 a day—much more than what other companies paid at that time. He also hoped that well-paid workers would be able to afford the cars he was making.

Other car builders adopted Ford's methods. Soon, the Ford Motor Company had competition from many other companies.

When Henry Ford died in 1947, he was one of the most famous people in the world. Factories of all kinds were using Ford's secret of success—the production line. And his company was one of the largest.

See also **automobile** and **production line.**

forest

A forest is an area where the main plants are trees. Most forests are large. They may cover millions of square kilometers. They provide homes for all sorts of living things. On a hike through a shady forest, you may find tiny wildflowers and interesting fungi. You will hear a variety of birdcalls, and perhaps catch a glimpse of a chipmunk, a rabbit, or even a deer. Turn over a rock, and you may find shiny beetles, wriggling worms, or a centipede. You may collect some nuts or berries. You may find a snakeskin left draped over a log or shrub.

Kinds of Forests   There are three main kinds of forests in North America.

Evergreen forests of cone-bearing trees are farthest north. They stretch across Canada and reach into the United States. Fingers of these forests follow the tall mountain ranges of the western part of the continent. Spruces, firs, and certain pines are common in evergreen forests.

Broadleaf forests are common in warmer areas, such as southern Canada and the eastern United States. These forests are made up of trees with broad leaves, such as maples, beeches, oaks, and hickories.

In the fall, broadleaf trees change color while cone-bearing trees stay green (below). Large trees shade the forest floor so that few plants can grow there. (right).

Temperate rain forests grow along the west coast of North America from northern California into Alaska. This kind of rain forest consists mainly of evergreen trees, such as the redwoods of California, Douglas firs of Washington, and Sitka spruces of Alaska. Temperatures in temperate rain forests are cool to cold. But these forests receive a lot of moisture from the Pacific Ocean.

Tropical rain forests, a fourth kind of forest, grow in areas near the equator. In tropical rain forests, it is warm to hot all year, and there is a lot of rain.

Not All Trees Are Forest Trees The kinds of forests are different in many ways, but they have some things in common. Trees that grow and reproduce in a forest share an important characteristic. They do not need a lot of sunlight to grow. When they sprout from a seed, they can grow well on the shady forest floor.

Not all trees have this characteristic. Many trees, such as aspens, can sprout and grow only in full sunlight. These trees grow on the edges of forests. They can also grow in forest areas where trees have fallen or been cut down. For a while, they get the sunlight they need. But in time, seeds of shade-loving trees sprout under these sun-loving trees. As the shade-loving trees grow, they replace the sun-loving trees.

Where Forests Grow The kind of forest that grows in an area is determined by the temperature and also by the amount of water that is available. Where temperatures are cold and most water arrives as snow, the forests are evergreen. Broadleaf forests grow in warmer areas that receive both rain and snow. They are most plentiful in areas that have four distinct seasons.

In tropical rain forests, it may rain every day. The northwestern rain forest is special. Winds blowing off the Pacific Ocean are filled with moisture. Soon after they reach the coast, the winds run into mountains. The mountains force the moist air upward. As

the air rises, it cools. The moisture in the air falls as rain or snow.

Where there is not enough water, there will be no forest at all. The plains region of North America and the North American desert do not have forests. There is not enough water.

Where temperatures are too cold, there are no forests, either. In the Far North of North America, there is lots of water in the soil, but there are no forests. It is so cold that the soil is frozen all year. The trees cannot use the frozen water. In summer, the water in the very top layer of soil may melt. But the only trees that can grow are those with very shallow roots, and they are too small to form a forest.

Soils of forests vary a great deal. The northern evergreen forests grow in thin soil that is poor in nutrients. Tropical rain forests, too, grow in fairly poor soil. All that rain washes the nutrients out of the soil. The deepest, richest forest soils are in broadleaf

Broadleaf trees grow in the valleys and evergreens grow on the slopes. On the highest places, no trees grow at all.

forests. There is not enough rain to wash all the nutrients away. Decaying leaves produce new nutrients for the soil.

Life in the Forest Each kind of forest is home to a different group of living things. Besides plants, mammals, and birds, there are millions of other creatures, some too small to be seen without a microscope. The soil in evergreen forests is covered with a thick layer of needles. Only a few kinds of plants can live on these needles. So evergreen forests do not have a lot of wildflowers and shrubs growing under the trees. But there are many flowers and shrubs in forest clearings. Moose, caribou, wolves, coyotes, snowshoe rabbits, and owls are large animals that live in evergreen forests. Mice, chipmunks, moles, shrews, and other small animals live on the forest floor. Besides owls, there are many smaller birds, including jays, grosbeaks, and grouse.

The broadleaf forest is more complex than the evergreen forest. It seems to have many layers. The first layer is the living things on the forest floor—wildflowers, fungi, ferns, and mosses. The next layer consists of shrubs—raspberry, rose, gooseberry, and many other kinds of bushes. Small trees make up the next layer. Some are small adult trees, such as dogwoods. Others are the young offspring of big trees in the forest.

The full-grown big trees make up the final layer. Usually, there are only a few kinds of these trees. In some places, they are oaks and hickories. In others, they are maples, beeches, and birches. Branches of neighboring trees may overlap. When the trees are in leaf, the leaves form a covering, called a *canopy*, over the whole forest. The canopy keeps the forest shady and cool on hot summer days.

Broadleaf forests are full of wildlife. Foxes, groundhogs, raccoons, opossums, skunks, hawks, and owls make their homes here. So do chipmunks, squirrels, mice, and wood rats. There are many songbirds in broadleaf forests. Chickadees, warblers, wrens, nuthatches, cardinals, and sparrows are only a few of the birds you might see. Toads and snakes are also present, as well as many different kinds of insects and worms.

The temperate rain forest is made up of towering evergreen trees. In some places, there is so much rain that mosses form deep mats over the forest floor. Vines creep around trees. Orchids, periwinkles, and other wildflowers grow here. Beavers and rabbits make their homes in this forest. So do hawks and many other birds. Insects are plentiful, especially in midsummer.

The tropical rain forest has more kinds of living things than any other natural community. Other forests have many trees, but only a few kinds. Tropical rain forests have many kinds of trees, but only a few of each kind. Also, unlike in the broadleaf forest, there is no bottom layer. Most of the life is in the high canopy.

Monkeys and brightly colored birds move among the branches. Insects of all kinds creep, crawl, and fly through this forest. Dozens of kinds of snakes live here, some in the trees. All these different living things make the tropical rain forest a colorful and noisy place.

Each kind of forest is special in its own way. Each has interesting things not found in the others. It is not hard to understand why we humans enjoy forests.

See also **biome; cone-bearing plant; evergreen tree; forestry; hardwood tree; rain forest;** and **tree.**

forestry

Forestry is the study of forests and how to take care of them. People who study forests are often called *foresters.* They manage and protect forests so we can continue to use and enjoy them.

Foresters learn about trees and how to grow them. They study soils and climates to understand how these things affect forests. They also study tree diseases and ways to combat them. When trees in a forest are dying, foresters can often find ways to save

A beaver has damaged this tree and may cut it down to help make a dam.

them, or to prevent other trees from getting sick.

Foresters need to understand how animals affect trees, too. They can tell which animals are in an area by looking at tree damage. They can tell if a tree has been cut down by a beaver. They recognize the work of a porcupine when they see a ring of bark taken off all the way around a tree. They know deer are present when they find shrubs and small trees with their leaves stripped.

Foresters also know which trees produce good wood for houses, furniture, paper, and other uses. They know which trees produce other things that people can use. Some trees produce nuts. Others produce sap, which we use for maple syrup. Turpentine and other useful fluids are produced from certain kinds of trees.

Foresters care for large forests so these products can be harvested like crops. They know how to cut down trees for lumber without destroying the forest. They have developed ways to replant cut areas with young trees to protect the forest soil from erosion.

Foresters know how long it takes for trees to grow large enough for people to use. They plan how many to cut, and when to cut them. In this way, they help make sure that

fossil

we do not use our forests faster than they can grow back.

If you have visited a national forest, you may have seen a sign that said "Land of Many Uses." Many forests have streams or lakes that are good for fishing. Some forests have useful minerals in their soil. Foresters plan ways to allow all of these resources to be used. They may build trails to favorite fishing areas. These trails let people enjoy all parts of the forest without harming it.

Foresters may work with miners to find safe ways of removing valuable minerals from the soil. They may have to let some trees be cut down. But they make sure that new, young trees are planted after the mining is completed.

Forestry also includes helping people learn about and enjoy forests through hiking, camping, and other activities.

See also **forest.**

---

fossil

Fossils are the remains of plants and animals that lived on the earth long ago. Nature has preserved these ancient remains by burying them in thick layers of rock. People are still finding fossils today.

These logs were once wood, but gradually turned to stone. They are a kind of fossil which we call *petrified wood.*

Each rock preserves a fossil—a print left by a plant or animal millions of years ago.

The oldest known fossils are over 3 billion years old. They are remains of bacteria and one-celled algae that lived in the sea. These show that there has been life on earth for a very long time. They also tell us a great deal about the history of the earth.

We have discovered fossils from many periods of earth's history up to the end of the last ice age, about 10,000 years ago. But scientists know that they may be "missing" fossil records for many periods and for many kinds of plants and animals. When plants and animals die, their remains usually decay before they can be covered by rock or protected in some other way.

Fossils can form in various ways. Some fossils form on the floor of a lake or shallow sea. Small particles called *sediment* fall through the water and cover a dead plant or animal. Other fossils form in swamps or tar pits, where bodies of plants or animals can sink into mud or tar. Sometimes, a volcanic eruption covers living things with ash. Animals may bury bones and then forget to dig them up. Insects sometimes get caught in juices that ooze from some trees. When the juices harden to a clear substance called *amber,* the insect is preserved as a fossil.

When a fossil is covered by sediment or mud, it still can change. After millions of years, the sediment or mud that encloses the bones will turn to rock. Water seeping through the rock may dissolve the bones, leaving empty places where they used to be. Or the bones may be replaced by different kinds of minerals. When that happens, the fossil is said to be *petrified.*

Animals without hard parts usually leave just outlines of themselves. A jellyfish, for example, might leave a thin film of carbon pressed between the layers of a rock.

These are not the only kinds of fossils that scientists look for. The hardened footprints of a creature such as a dinosaur are also fossils. They tell scientists interesting things about how the creatures lived and died. Even fossil eggs have been found, some of them with embryo dinosaurs inside.

See also **animals, prehistoric** and **earth history.**

Foster, Stephen C.

Stephen C. Foster was a great American songwriter. He wrote hundreds of tunes and words for songs in the 1800s. We still sing many of them today.

Foster was born in 1826 in western Pennsylvania. He was picking out tunes on a guitar before he was old enough to go to school. When he was 16, he wrote his first song. When he was only 20, he wrote "Oh! Susanna," which has been an American favorite ever since.

When Foster was 24, he married Jane McDowell. In the next few years, he wrote some of his most famous songs. "Jeanie with the Light Brown Hair" was for his wife. His most popular song of all is "Old Folks at Home,"

also known as "Way Down Upon the Swanee River."

Foster's simple words and tunes were easy for people to learn and sing. The songs also expressed feelings that most people recognized and felt themselves.

Foster and his songs were very popular, but Foster himself was very unhappy. He quarreled with his friends. He died at the age of 37 in New York City, alone and poor.

See also **music.**

Four-H Clubs

Four-H, or 4-H, is an organization for young people aged 9 to 19. It began in the United States in the early 1900s. Its members were farm children. Four-H helped teach them farm skills needed for raising crops and animals. They often exhibited their prize animals and vegetables at state and county fairs.

Today, 4-H activities are much more varied, though many 4-H members still have fun learning farm skills. Most members do not live on farms. About 3½ million young people in the United States alone belong to 4-H, and there are 4-H clubs in about 80 other countries. They work together on all sorts of projects, most having to do with agriculture, health, or community service. Many 4-H projects are now connected with

Stephen Foster wrote many songs in the 1800s that Americans still sing today.

We celebrate the Fourth of July, the birthday of the United States, with fireworks. The Statue of Liberty, a symbol of American freedom, is in the background.

city life. Members may plant trees—or learn to sew, cook, make household repairs, make car repairs, or manage money.

The four *H*'s stand for *head, heart, hands,* and *health.* They come from the Four-H pledge: "I pledge my head to clearer thinking, my heart to greater loyalty, my hands to larger service, and my health to better living for my club, my community, my country, and my world." The Four-H symbol is a four-leaf clover with an *H* on each leaf.

Fourth of July

The Fourth of July is the birthday of the United States. On July 4, 1776, the American colonies declared their independence from Great Britain and adopted the Declaration of Independence. The colonies still had to fight the Revolutionary War to become fully independent. But ever since 1776, Americans have celebrated their liberty on the Fourth of July. Other names for the holiday are Independence Day and July Fourth.

The Fourth of July is celebrated in the United States and in all its territories and possessions. Many businesses are closed, no mail is delivered, and government offices are closed. People often gather for cookouts and picnics. Many cities and towns have parades. Marching bands, fire and police departments, and scout groups join in the celebration. In states that were the original 13 colonies, marchers often dress up in colonial-style clothing. They may play fifes and drums, like the military bands of the Revolutionary War. Some cities and towns have concerts, shows, and sports events. Radio and television stations may play patriotic songs for the Fourth of July.

Fireworks have always been a part of the Fourth of July celebration. Some communities have elaborate fireworks displays. Some of these displays are shown on television for people who cannot see them in person.

Two of the biggest Fourth of July celebrations took place for the Centennial (100th birthday of the nation) and the Bicentennial (200th birthday). For the Centennial, the city of Philadelphia held a great fair called the Centennial Exposition. It lasted seven months and featured many U.S. products and inventions.

On the Bicentennial, there was a huge celebration at the Statue of Liberty. A great Fourth of July party was held throughout the nation.

See also **Declaration of Independence.**

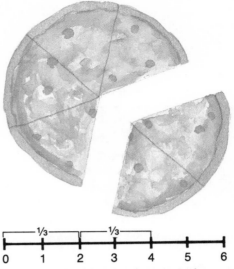

This pizza is cut into six equal pieces called sixths. Four-sixths of the pizza is the same as two-thirds of it.

fox

Foxes are members of the dog family. Most of them look like small dogs, but foxes have bushy tails. They live in almost every part of the world, from cold Arctic regions to hot deserts. While the young, called *pups,* are growing up, foxes live in families. Foxes hunt at night, alone or in pairs. They never form packs.

Foxes eat mice, insects, birds, rabbits, and frogs. Sometimes, they kill chickens. When foxes catch more food than they need, they save some. They dig holes with their front paws, drop in the food, and cover it with soil. When food is scarce, they dig up the hidden food.

Foxes are very clever. They can avoid traps people set for them. If a dog is tracking them, they will break their trail of scent by swimming in water or mixing in with cattle. Foxes can even play "dead."

The most common fox is the red fox. It is found throughout North America, Europe, and Asia. It has reddish fur. Like most other foxes, it digs a den in the ground. A den may have many rooms and entrances. The fox escapes from enemies by running into its den. It stores food there. It also uses one room in the den as a nursery for its pups.

See also **dog family.**

A red fox has a keen sense of hearing which helps it hunt prey.

fraction

If you break a cupcake into two equal parts, each part is called a half—1/2. Each half is a *fraction* of the whole cupcake. If another cupcake is broken into four parts, each part is a fourth—1/4. Three of these parts is three-fourths—3/4.

The word *fraction* comes from the Latin word *fractus,* meaning "broken." The bottom number in a fraction tells you how many parts a thing has been broken into. It is called the *denominator.* For example, in the fraction 3/4 (three-fourths), 4 is the denominator. It tells how many equal parts make up the whole. The top number of a fraction tells you how many of those parts you have. It is called the *numerator.* In 3/4, 3 is the numerator.

It is easy to think of a fraction as a number, but a fraction is not really a number. It is a name for a number. Think of a pizza cut into six pieces. You have four of the six pieces. The fraction describing what you have is 4/6. But 4/6 is the same amount as that described by the fraction 2/3. Two different fractions can name the same amount.

One way to show the number named by a fraction is by using a number line. On a number line, the fractions 2/3 and 4/6 both fall at the same place between 0 and 1.

See also **decimal; number;** and **numeral.**

France

Capital: Paris
Area: 221,207 square miles (572,926 square kilometers)
Population (1985): about 55,041,000
Official language: French

France is the largest country in Western Europe. It is about twice the size of the state of Colorado. In all of Europe, only the European part of the Soviet Union covers a larger area.

France is a nation of great variety. Its population—more than 54 million people—is a mix of many different races and religions. Most people in France are Roman Catholics. There are also many French Jews and Muslims. France has long had ties with North Africa, where most people are Muslims.

Land   The land of France is as varied as its people. Its northern border runs along

France is famous for delicious foods, including rich pastry desserts.

Belgium and the English Channel. The north is mostly flat land or rolling hills. Paris, the capital, is in the north. More than 2 million people live in Paris. Several million more live nearby.

The central part of France has rich farmlands and river valleys. Much of the land is used for growing grapes to make wine. The French make some of the best wines in the world. Much of it is sold in other countries, including the United States.

The southeastern region is a land of high mountains and lakes. These mountains, the Alps, spread into the neighboring countries of Germany, Switzerland, and Italy. The highest peak in the Alps is in France. It is called Mont Blanc, which means "white mountain" in French. (*See* **Alps**.)

To the southwest is a chain of mountains called the Pyrenees (PEER-uh-neez), along France's border with Spain. France's famous Riviera lies between the Alps and the Pyrenees. The Riviera is France's southern coast on the Mediterranean Sea. Its beaches and cities are popular vacation spots.

History   France has a long, colorful history. Some of the world's greatest military leaders have ruled the country. The Roman emperor Julius Caesar took over the lands of France between 58 B.C. and 51 B.C. In ancient times, the territory was known as Gaul.

The Romans ruled France for more than 500 years. Then tribes from Germany streamed into the region. One of these tribes was the Franks. They overthrew the Roman rulers in 486. France got its name from the Franks.

The Franks ruled for centuries. The greatest of the Frankish kings was Charlemagne (SHAR-luh-main). In fact, his name means "Charles the Great." He was crowned king of France in 800. He brought much of Western Europe under his rule, too. After he died, later kings lost much of that territory.

In the 1600s, another great king, Louis XIV, ruled for more than 60 years. France became very powerful, and it again ruled some other countries. (*See* **Louis XIV**.)

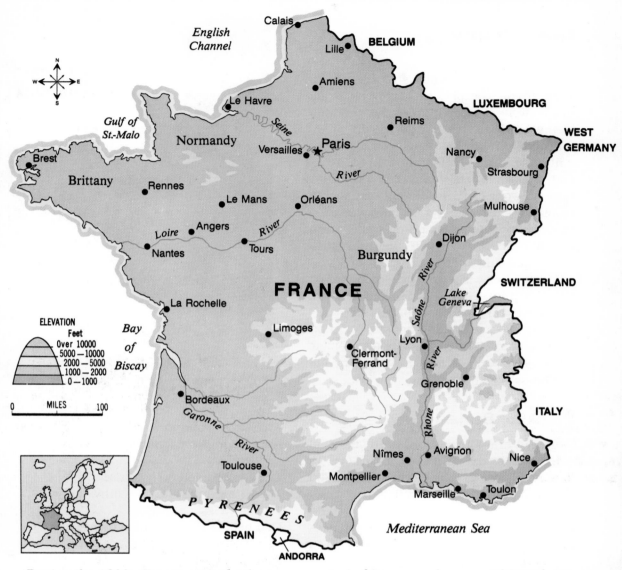

During the 1600s, France started colonies in North America. The largest were in Canada. Others were in what is now the United States, along the Great Lakes and the Mississippi River.

In the late 1700s, France lost many of its colonies. At home, the French people were unhappy with their king, Louis XVI. The king's court and the nobles were spending more and more money. Meanwhile, the common people struggled to survive and poor people starved.

On July 14, 1789, French revolutionaries stormed the Bastille, a large prison in Paris. They freed all the prisoners and soon took over the entire city. That was the beginning of the French Revolution. In 1792, the revolutionaries overthrew the king. They took control of France and soon established a republic—a free government chosen by the people. The French still celebrate July 14, Bastille Day, as a national holiday. (*See* **French Revolution**.)

The French Revolution was very cruel. Its leaders killed the king and queen and many other people. Within a few years, a military leader took control of the government. His name was Napoleon, and he became one of the great generals in world history. He wanted to bring all of Europe under his rule, and he almost succeeded. But in 1815, a British Army defeated Napoleon's army near Waterloo, a town in Belgium, and Napoleon fell from power. (*See* **Napoleon**.)

After Napoleon, France was involved in other wars. Between 1870 and 1945, huge

printing & publishing

armies fought on French soil three times. Many French people died. Many cities and towns were destroyed, then later rebuilt. (*See* **World War I** and **World War II.**)

People France has long been an important center of art and literature. In the 1800s and 1900s, artists from many countries came to work in Paris. Among the most famous French painters were the *impressionists.* They painted colorful scenes from everyday life. (*See* **Renoir, Pierre-Auguste** and **Degas, Edgar.**)

Today, France is a wealthy, productive nation. Its people enjoy a standard of living about equal to that of the United States. Perhaps the most important industry in France is auto-making. But France is also famous for its perfumes, its fashion designers, and its excellent food.

Franklin was a publisher, inventor and scientist. He also was a government leader.

Franklin, Benjamin

Benjamin Franklin was one of the most talented and energetic people in history. He lived for almost 85 years, from 1706 to 1790. He was a printer, a writer, a newspaper publisher, a scientist, an inventor, and a leader of his country. In fact, Franklin helped to establish that country, the new United States of America.

Franklin was born in Boston, in the colony of Massachusetts. He was the youngest son in a large, poor family. When he was ten, Ben left school to work in the family's shop making soap and candles. He soon found his job dull. He loved to read newspapers and books, so he asked to work in a printing shop run by his brother. There Ben learned how to set type, run a printing press, and write for a newspaper.

When Franklin was 17, he quarreled with his brother and ran away, first to New York City and then to Philadelphia. Within a few years, he was writing and printing his own newspaper. The *Pennsylvania Gazette* became one of the most widely read newspapers in the colonies. Franklin also began to publish a kind of yearly calendar called *Poor*

Richard's Almanack. Many of Poor Richard's sayings are famous even today.

Early to bed and early to rise
Makes a man healthy, wealthy, and wise.

God helps those who help themselves.

An ounce of prevention is worth a pound of cure.

While he was building his business, Franklin was also helping his city. He began both the first lending library and the first volunteer fire department in the United States. He helped raise money for a city hospital. He also helped begin a school that later became the University of Pennsylvania.

Franklin was interested in solving everyday problems, too. He noticed that his fireplace did not heat his room very well. The fireplace burned a lot of wood, but too much heat went up the chimney. Franklin built a new kind of stove that fit into the fireplace. The "Franklin stove," made of iron, gave more heat but burned less wood than other stoves. Stoves like this are still made

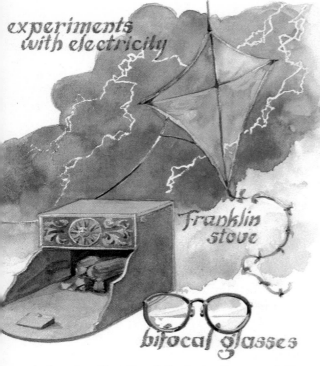

experiments with electricity

Franklin stove

bifocal glasses

today. Another Franklin invention was bifocal eyeglasses. People using them can see something at a distance or read something close.

Lightning interested Franklin. He believed it was caused by electricity in the clouds. To test his idea, he flew a kite during a lightning storm. He fastened a pointed wire to the kite, and attached to the wire a silk string with a metal key tied to its ends. Lightning struck the wire, traveled down the wet string, and made the key spark. Franklin's experiment showed that lightning is a form of electricity. The next two people who tried it were killed.

One useful result of his discovery was the lightning rod. Lightning often struck barns and houses and set them afire. Hoping to prevent this, Franklin put a metal rod on his roof. A metal wire connected the rod to the ground. In a storm, lightning struck the rod, not the house. The metal wire conducted the electricity safely into the ground. Once people realized lightning rods worked, they quickly started using them.

By the time he was 42, Franklin's printing business was a success. He had more time to work on other things. He became director of the postal service for the American colonies. His plans helped get letters delivered quickly. He also served as a member of the Pennsylvania Assembly, which helped to govern the colony.

The British government ruled the colonies and collected taxes from the colonists. The colonists thought the taxes were too high and that some of the laws were unfair. The colonists of Pennsylvania sent Franklin to Great Britain to present their complaints. He spent 18 years there trying to persuade the British to govern the colonists more fairly. But the British and the colonists continued to quarrel.

When Franklin returned home in 1775, the Revolutionary War between Britain and the colonies was just beginning. He became a member of the Second Continental Congress, which decided that the colonies should be free of British rule. In 1776, Franklin signed the Declaration of Independence. In this document, the colonists announced that they were independent of Britain.

Franklin returned to Europe. He asked France if they would help the colonies in their war against Britain. The French agreed to send weapons and supplies for the American armies. The French navy also helped the colonists in their fight to win the Revolutionary War.

Franklin stayed in France to help write the peace treaty between Britain and a new country, the United States. He returned home in 1785. In 1787, the state of Pennsylvania sent him to the Constitutional Convention to help write a constitution for the United States. Men from the different states argued over what the Constitution should say. Franklin was 81 years old and often sick. But he helped the men settle their differences. The Constitution is still the supreme law of the United States.

Benjamin Franklin died in 1790. Two centuries later, people still think of him as one of America's most remarkable men.

See also **Constitution of the United States; Declaration of Independence; Revolutionary War;** and **United States history.**

French and Indian War

The French and Indian War was actually a war between France and Britain over control of a large part of North America. The war began in 1754 and ended in 1763, just 13 years before the American Revolution. Fighting took place in the colonies and in Canada. The colonists fought on the British side. Most American Indians helped the French.

Both countries claimed ownership of the same land. The French began settling in Canada along the St. Lawrence River in the early 1600s. They had trading posts around the Great Lakes and along the Ohio and Mississippi rivers. Here they bought furs from Indian trappers. The British, too, were settling in Canada. They had farming and fishing villages along the Atlantic coast, and trading posts around Hudson Bay. Both the British and the French claimed the land west of the 13 colonies.

A group of Virginia businessmen wanted to divide the Ohio Valley into small farms. The forests, where thousands of fur-bearing animals lived, would have to be cleared. To protect their own fur trade, the French built forts along Lake Erie and the Ohio River.

Bad feelings increased between the British and French, and war seemed certain. In April 1754, a group of soldiers commanded by 22-year-old George Washington left Virginia for the Ohio River. They built Fort Necessity. It is just south of France's Fort Duquesne, where Pittsburgh stands today.

In July, the French and their Indian allies attacked the British fort. Washington and his men were outnumbered and had to retreat to Virginia. The British had lost the first battle of the French and Indian War.

The next year, Britain sent General Edward Braddock to take charge of the war against the French. With him came several regiments of British soldiers, called "redcoats" because of their red-coated uniforms.

Braddock and his redcoats marched to Fort Duquesne. With them were George Washington and the Virginia militia. About 10 miles south of Fort Duquesne, they were surprised by French and Indian troops. Their bright coats made the British soldiers easy targets for French and Indian marksmen hiding behind trees and rocks. Braddock knew nothing about this way of fighting. As soon as he ordered a group of soldiers to stand and fight, the enemy would vanish into the forest.

In that battle, about 1,000 of the 1,500 British soldiers were killed or wounded. Braddock himself lost his life. Washington and his men escaped. The British and colonial side had lost again.

The map shows French forts along the Great Lakes and St. Lawrence River. British settlements were in New England, New York, and Pennsylvania. Right, George Washington fought for the British in western Pennsylvania.

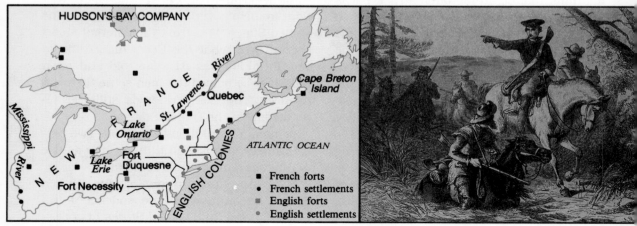

British troops climbed cliffs from the St. Lawrence River to the Plains of Abraham, just outside the French city of Quebec. They defeated the French, ending the war.

Over the years, the battles continued. One side won, and then the other side won. Gradually the tide turned in favor of the British. They captured the French fort on Cape Breton Island off Canada's eastern coast. This helped the British navy cut off the enemy's supplies from France. Then they captured a French fort on Lake Ontario. Fort Duquesne and the rest of the Ohio Valley were cut off from French Canada. The French blew up Fort Duquesne and retreated.

By 1759, the stage was set for a British and colonial attack on the French-Canadian center—Quebec. Victory there could mean the end of French resistance. But Quebec seemed an impossible fortress to take. It sat on the Plains of Abraham, high above the St. Lawrence River. Its guns were aimed down the steep cliffs. About 140 British ships, carrying 9,000 troops, waited in the St. Lawrence, just beyond the range of the guns.

Marquis de Montcalm commanded the French forces. He had won impressive victories against the British, and he felt well protected in the Quebec fortress.

General James Wolfe commanded the British forces. Looking at the rocky cliffs, he wondered how his men could attack. Then he discovered a steep, narrow path that zigzagged up the cliff. On the night of September 12, 1759, he ordered his men into long rowboats. In the darkness, they silently slipped under the French guns and rowed toward the path. All night, they climbed single file toward the fortress.

At dawn, the British surprised the French on the Plains of Abraham. A brief battle followed. Before he could know the battle was lost, Montcalm was killed. Wolfe, too, was killed, but he knew he had won.

The fall of Quebec marked the end of fighting in the French and Indian War. But the peace treaty was not signed until four years later, in 1763. France had to give up all its claims to Canada and to land east of the Mississippi River. Britain and the colonies had gained what they wanted—dominance in eastern North America.

See also **Washington, George; France;** and **English history.**

French Guiana, *see* South America

French Revolution

France in the late 1700s was a country in trouble. The king and the noble families held all the power. But the money to run the government came mostly from high taxes paid by the middle class and the common people. The nation could barely pay its bills, but King Louis XVI was a weak ruler who refused to make any real changes.

This was also a time when many thinkers were writing about equality and the idea that people had a right to rule themselves. The United States won its freedom from England and became the first nation to put these ideas into practice. Many people in France felt their country should follow this example and create a new government.

By 1789, there was much unrest. King Louis XVI called a meeting of France's assembly. When its members gathered in Paris, many demanded that changes be made. This was the beginning of the French Revolution, which lasted until 1799.

When the king tried to cut the meeting short, the people rebelled. They seized control of a prison called the Bastille on July 14, 1789. A National Assembly was formed, and a constitution was written. It listed the rights of the people and limited the king's powers. People seized land and property belonging to the upper classes.

Other European kings worried that revolutionary ideas might spread to their own countries. In 1792, France found itself at war with Prussia and Austria. The French people thought that Louis XVI was plotting with other kings against France. The king was then put into prison, and his powers were taken away.

A Committee of Public Safety was formed in 1793 to watch over the country. The committee members actually ran the government. During this period, known as the "Reign of Terror," anybody suspected of being an enemy of France was jailed or killed. Thousands were sent to the *guillotine,* a machine that beheaded people. After the king

On July 14, 1789, the people of Paris stormed a prison called the Bastille and began the French Revolution. In France, July 14 is Bastille Day, a national holiday.

tried to escape, he and the queen, Marie Antoinette, were guillotined. Finally, the French were sickened by the violence, and turned against those who had led it. France soon fell under the rule of a single strong leader, Napoleon. (*See* **Napoleon**.)

Sigmund Freud suggested new ways to understand thoughts and feelings.

Freud, Sigmund

Sigmund Freud was a doctor who was interested in how the human mind works. His research was important in the development of *psychology*, the study of mind and behavior. It also had great influence in the field of medicine called *pyschiatry*, which treats mental illness.

Freud was born in 1856 and died in 1939. He lived most of his life in Vienna, Austria. Freud believed that our lives are strongly affected by the *unconscious*—thoughts and feelings that we are not aware of having. For example, you may unconsciously feel jealous of your best friend because he or she is a better student. Freud said the unconscious could be revealed in many ways. One way is through dreams. You may dream that something bad happens to your best friend.

Freud also said that our unconscious feelings can cause problems for us. He worked out a system called *psychoanalysis* to discover and treat such problems. Using *free*

association, a patient talks to a doctor about whatever comes to mind. This often helps a patient understand and deal with problems and lead a happier life.

See also **psychiatry** and **psychology.**

friction

Every time you ride in a car, you are using the force of friction. Friction is the force that acts between two things that rub together.

Friction is very important in everyday life. Tire designers want tires to have lots of friction with the road. Without friction, a car's tires would just spin in the same place when the driver tried to start moving. Drivers also need friction to help them stop. Without friction, a car would just skid when the driver put on the brakes. It would not even slow down!

Friction produces heat. If you slide down a rope, friction can burn your hands. If you rub two dry sticks together for a long time, you can even start a fire. The head of a match has chemicals that catch fire when the friction of striking the match produces enough heat.

Friction can be very helpful, but it can also be harmful. It slows down moving machinery. The moving parts heat up and wear out because of the friction. We often use oil and other substances to reduce friction in machines and to keep them running smoothly. We also use special cooling systems to keep the machinery cool. Car radiators do this important job.

A running shoe grips the ground, providing friction that keeps a runner from slipping.

A tree frog can change colors to blend into its surroundings.

frogs and toads

Frogs and toads are *amphibians*. The name means "those living a double life"—a life in water and a life on land. Frogs and toads lay their eggs in water. When the eggs hatch, they look like fish. They have streamlined bodies, a long tail, and gills. These young animals are called *larvae,* or *tadpoles.* They live in water and slowly *metamorphose* —change—into adult frogs and toads. They develop legs and lungs, and the tail and gills disappear. After these changes are complete, the animals are ready to live on land. (*See* **amphibian.**)

Stand near a lake or river on a summer night and listen. You will hear male frogs and toads calling to the females. Sometimes, they are very, very noisy. The spring peeper is a tiny frog, no bigger than the end of your thumb. But its call can be heard almost 1.5 kilometers (1 mile) away!

The male spring peeper takes a deep breath so that air goes into his lungs. Then he closes his mouth and forces out that air. As the air moves over the vocal cords, they vibrate and make sounds. Some male frogs have a *vocal sac*—a special pouch under the throat. This pouch fills with air and makes the sound louder.

It is not easy to tell frogs and toads apart. But there are differences between them. Most frogs have longer bodies than toads and are not as heavy. Frogs are excellent jumpers. They usually have long, powerful back legs. A toad's legs are shorter. Toads do more hopping than jumping. Frogs have moist, smooth skin, and toads have dry, bumpy skin. The bumps look like warts, but they are actually poison glands. You cannot get warts by touching a toad. Most frogs live in water, while most toads live on land.

Despite these differences, some kinds of frogs are more closely related to toads than to other frogs. And some toads are more closely related to frogs than to other toads. Scientists call all these animals "frogs," and so will we here.

leopard frog

egg mass

larva

green frog

bullfrog

common toad

Toads usually have dry, bumpy skin (left). Frogs are often green and have smooth, moist skin (right). Frogs and toads use long, sticky tongues to catch insects (below).

Frost makes beautiful patterns on a window (above). At right, frost forms on a can of frozen juice.

Insects are a frog's main food. A frog has a wide mouth and a long tongue with a rough, sticky tip. The frog can flick out its tongue with lightning speed to catch a flying insect. The sticky tip holds the insect while the frog draws in its tongue. Frogs have huge appetites. Scientists once saw a frog eat 53 mosquitoes in one minute!

There are about 2,000 known kinds of frogs. The greatest variety of frogs live in the tropics. The leopard frog and bullfrog are the most common kinds in North America.

About 25 kinds of tree frogs live in the United States. Tree frogs are small—less than 5 centimeters (2 inches). Sticky pads on their toes make it easy for them to climb trees. But not all tree frogs live in trees. The spring peeper, which lives in eastern North America, stays on the ground. The Pacific tree frog of western North America is usually found on the ground or in bushes.

Many frogs are protected by their coloring. They blend into their surroundings and may not be noticed by enemies and prey. Most frogs are dull green or brown. Some can change from one color to another, or make their color get lighter or darker. Others are brightly colored and may have beautiful patterns. Many of these colorful frogs are poisonous. The bright colors warn enemies to keep away. (*See* **camouflage.**)

frost

The cold, sugary-looking coating on the outside of a frozen juice can is frost. If you live in a cold climate, you have probably seen a dusting of frost on the grass in the morning. We say "Jack Frost paid us a visit, leaving ice crystals on everything he touched." But that is not the real story.

Air contains invisible water vapor—water in the form of a gas. Warm air can hold more water vapor than cool air. When air is cooled past its *dew point,* its water vapor condenses into liquid water droplets. If the temperature falls below 0° C (32° F), the droplets freeze and ice crystals "grow" on them. Sometimes, the water vapor changes directly into ice crystals.

Frost forms best on clear, windless nights. The earth cools quickly on such nights. As air near the earth cools below its dew point, frost begins to form on grass, leaves, and other cold surfaces. On cloudy nights, clouds hold heat near the earth. If the weather is windy, the air does not stay near cold surfaces long enough to reach its dew point.

Farmers worry about frosts because plants may freeze and die. In groves of citrus trees, farmers build small fires and use fans to keep the air moving.

See also **dew.**

Fruits include nuts and corn. We can preserve fruits by making jam or jelly or by drying them. A raisin is a dried grape.

fruit

A fruit is the part of a flowering plant that develops from the flower. It usually contains the plant's seeds. Most people think of fruits as sweet, juicy foods that grow on trees, vines, or bushes—apples, pears, peaches, apricots, plums, melons, grapes, berries, and citrus. But to a scientist, corn, holly berries, tomatoes, almonds, cucumbers, and olives are fruits, too.

Fruits as Food Fruits are important foods for people and for many animals. They provide vitamins and minerals. Citrus fruits—oranges, lemons, limes, and grapefruit—are rich in vitamin C. Bananas and oranges contain potassium, an important mineral. Fruits also provide fiber, which people need to stay healthy.

Fruits are eaten in many ways. Most fruits can be eaten raw. Some can also be cooked. We make fruits into jams, jellies, and preserves, or into pies. Fruit juices are another way of enjoying fruits.

People have found ways to store fruits for use during times when they are not available fresh. Many fruits are canned to be eaten out of season. Some people do canning at home. Drying fruits is an old way of keeping them. Raisins are dried grapes, and prunes are dried plums. Some fresh fruits can be kept longer than others. Apples can last for almost a year if they are kept cold.

Fruits and Seeds Fruits help plants spread their seeds to places where they can grow. Before the seeds can sprout, they must find a place with good soil and the right amount of sun, shade, and moisture. They cannot reach such a place by themselves. They must be carried there.

Sweet, fleshy fruits attract hungry animals. Often, an animal eats the seeds as well as the fruit. The seeds pass through the animal's digestive system and drop to the ground with wastes. Other fruits, such as cockleburs, have little hooks on them. The hooks catch in the fur of passing animals or the clothing of passing humans. Later, when these fruits are brushed off, they may land on soil where they can grow. The fruits of maple trees have lightweight wings, and the fruits of milkweed have a lightweight puff. These fruits can be carried great distances by the wind.

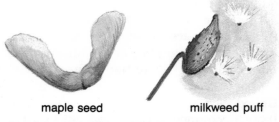

maple seed   milkweed puff

Maples and milkweed plants have fruits that will be carried far in the wind.

Growing Fruits Fruits grow on trees, bushes, woody vines, and nonwoody plants. At one time, all these plants grew wild. They usually produced small fruits. Farmers began raising the wild plants as crops. They used seeds from the best fruits for later crops. Soon they were growing plants that produced larger, tastier, juicier fruits.

Farmers also cultivate fruits by *cross-pollination*. They take the pollen from one variety of plant and place it in the flower of another variety. The seeds that result will be a cross between the two kinds of plants. Farmers plan the crosses so that the new

graft   cutting

Farmers can reproduce a plant by grafting (left) or by planting a cutting (right).

seeds will grow into plants that bear especially tasty and attractive fruits.

Some fruit trees are not grown from seeds. This is because some trees grown from seed do not produce fruit exactly like the fruit of their parent plants. For example, if a farmer wants an apple tree that produces good fruit, he or she cannot rely on apples grown from the seed of a good apple tree. Instead, the farmer *grafts* an apple of a good variety, such as the McIntosh, onto the roots of another plant. The McIntosh branch is slipped into a cut just above the roots of the other plant. When the branch and the cut grow together, the branch continues to produce McIntosh apples. Later, a branch from this new tree can be grafted on another root to get another McIntosh tree. All McIntosh trees are exactly alike, just as all Red Delicious apple trees are alike. The McIntosh trees may grow differently because of different roots or different soil. But they are still branches of the original McIntosh tree, and they all produce McIntosh apples. (*See* **apple.**)

Other fruit plants are started from *cuttings.* Stems or branches are cut from good fruit producers and are put into damp soil. They send down roots and begin to grow. When the cuttings mature, they produce fruit just like their parent plants. By growing plants from grafts and cuttings, farmers are able to control the variety and quality of the fruit. (*See* **plant breeding.**)

Kinds of Fruits There are two ways to classify the many kinds of fruits. Since each kind grows best in a particular climate, fruits may be grouped by climate. Some fruits grow well only in tropical climates. They require sunshine, warmth, and lots of rain. Tropical fruits include bananas, pineapples, papayas, and mangoes.

Subtropical fruits require mild or warm temperatures and light rainfall. Citrus fruits, figs, dates, olives, and avocados are subtropical fruits. They grow well in the warmer parts of the United States—California, Florida, Arizona, and Texas. Many of these fruits also grow well in parts of Mexico, the Middle East, northern Africa, and southern Europe.

Temperate fruits — such as cherries, quince, strawberries, and cranberries—need cold winters and warm summers. Some temperate fruit plants—such as apple and pear trees—must freeze in the winter in order to blossom in the spring.

FRUITS GROW IN DIFFERENT CLIMATES

tropical

papaya   banana   mango   pineapple

subtropical

orange   lemon   fig   date   avocado

temperate

cherry   apple   pear strawberry

TYPES OF FRUIT

simple
sunflower · acorn · bean · wheat · drupes · plum · cherry · grape · tomato · blueberry

aggregate
raspberry flower · raspberry · blackberry

multiple
fig flower · pineapple · fig

accessory
strawberry flower · strawberry · pomes · apple · pear

Fruits may also be classified according to the way they develop. This way, fruits fall into four classes—simple, aggregate, multiple, and accessory fruits.

All fruits develop from flower parts called *ovaries,* which contain the seeds. A *simple fruit* forms from a single ovary. Some simple fruits are dry. Beans, acorns, wheat, milkweed, and sunflower seeds are examples of dry simple fruits. Some split open and others remain closed. People often think of dry simple fruits as nuts or seeds.

Other simple fruits are called *drupes.* They have a single seed surrounded by juicy flesh. Drupes include peaches, plums, cherries, dates, and olives.

Another kind of simple fruit is the *berry.* These fruits have soft, juicy flesh. Inside are many seeds. Grapes, tomatoes, bananas, watermelons, blueberries, and citrus fruits are berries. (*See* **berries.**)

Aggregate fruits develop from several ovaries within a single flower. Raspberries and blackberries are aggregate fruits, not berries.

Multiple fruits develop from a cluster of flowers. The flowers' separate ovaries grow together. Pineapples and figs are examples of multiple fruits.

Accessory fruits are fruits with fleshy parts that form not from the ovary but from other parts of the flowering plant. Apples and pears are accessory fruits called *pomes.* Pomes have cores with seeds. The true fruit of these plants is this core. The strawberry is an accessory fruit, too. Each "seed" on the strawberry is a complete fruit. The fleshy part of the strawberry develops from the base of the flower, not from the ovary.

fuel

How are gasoline and pizza alike? Both are kinds of fuel. Gasoline is the fuel that powers your car. Pizza—like other foods—is a fuel that powers your body.

A fuel is a substance that can be used to produce heat. For thousands of years, wood was the most important fuel. People turned to *fossil fuels* when there was not enough wood to meet new energy needs.

Fossil fuels were once living things. The remains of bacteria, protists, fungi, plants, and animals all contain carbon-based chemicals. Heat and pressure over millions of years changed these carbon-based chemicals into oil, coal, or natural gas.

Petroleum—also called oil—is the fossil fuel we use most. We use it to make gasoline, diesel fuel, airplane fuel, and heating fuel.

Fossil fuels are becoming harder to find. So people are experimenting with other energy sources, such as nuclear fuels. Most nuclear fuels are made from the metal uranium. These fuels are used to power some electric power plants and submarines.

See also **energy; solar energy; coal; oil; gas, natural; gasoline;** and **nuclear power.**

Fulton, Robert

Robert Fulton is famous for building the first successful steamboat. He was born in Pennsylvania in 1765. At first, he wanted to be an artist. In his early twenties, he sailed to England to study painting. But once in Europe, he became more interested in science and engineering.

Fulton began studying ideas for steamboats. He built several models the size of toys. Finally, he built a model that worked. The U.S. minister to France, Robert Livingston, saw the model. He asked Fulton to build a full-size steamboat that could carry passengers up and down the Hudson River in New York State.

On August 17, 1807, Fulton's steamboat started on its first successful voyage. Its steam engine turned big paddle wheels. The paddles moved the boat up the Hudson River from New York City to Albany. Fulton's steamboat carried 40 passengers on that first trip. It was later named the *Clermont.* But people had already started calling it "Fulton's Folly" because they thought it would never be a practical means of transportation. They were wrong.

Robert Fulton did not invent the steamboat, but he did build the *Clermont,* the first really practical boat that traveled on steam power.

fungus

By the time Fulton died, in 1815, steamships were carrying passengers and cargo up and down most of the country's big rivers. Within 25 years, steamships were regularly crossing the Atlantic Ocean.

See also **steam engine** and **ship.**

fungus

A mushroom is a familiar kind of fungus. It belongs to a kingdom of living things called *fungi.* Scientists used to think fungi were plants. But fungi differ from plants in many ways.

One difference is that a fungus cannot make its own food. It usually gets its food from dead or decaying matter. A fungus sprouts and grows on this material. As the fungus grows, it releases chemicals into the material. The chemicals digest the material so the fungus can feed on it.

Most fungi are formed by long threads called *hyphae* that grow close together. Fungi reproduce by means of tiny, dustlike cells called *spores.* Each fungus releases its spores into the air. If they land in a suitable place, they sprout. A sprout grows new hyphae that form a new fungus.

Many fungi live most of their lives underground but send up a fruiting stalk to reproduce. The mushrooms we see growing in the woods or on a lawn are fruiting stalks. If you have ever walked through the woods and stepped on a puffball mushroom, you probably saw it release a puff of dust. The "dust" was the puffball's spores.

The fungus family includes molds, mushrooms, yeasts. One fungus is the cause of athlete's foot!

Mushrooms are only one kind of fungus. There are many others. Brightly colored *bracket fungi* grow on tree trunks. Molds that grow on bread or decaying fruit are fungi. Yeast, used in baking, is a one-celled fungus.

Some fungi cause damage or disease. Smuts and rusts are fungi that damage crops. Ringworm and athlete's foot are diseases caused by fungi. One beautiful red-and-white mushroom, the *Amanita,* contains a poison deadly to humans.

Fungi are useful in nature. By using dead material for food, they help recycle it. They also release some of their food into the soil. Plants and other organisms use it for their own growth.

People use fungi in many ways. Some fungi produce antibiotics that are used to treat infections and diseases. Yeasts are used in baking and in making beer. Some fungi are added to cheeses to give a special flavor. Mushrooms are eaten raw or cooked.

CAUTION: Only an expert can tell which mushrooms are safe to eat. Never take even a small taste of a mushroom that you find growing.

See also **mushroom; mold;** and **yeast.**

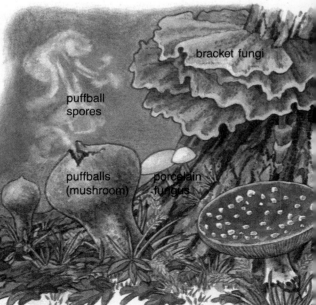

bracket fungi

puffball spores

puffballs (mushroom)

porcelain fungus

fly agaric (mushroom)

green mold on oranges

coprinus fungus

A raccoon's fur
has layers
of different
kinds of hair.

fur

Fur is the hair that covers some animals. It is a combination of long, stiff guard hairs and short, thick underfur. The oily guard hairs shed water, and the underfur keeps the animal warm.

The thickness and color of an animal's fur change with the seasons. The fur of mink, fox, beaver, and sable is thickest in winter. This is when they are hunted and trapped. In winter, an ermine's fur is snow-white with a black tip on the tail. In summer, its fur turns brown.

All fur used to come from wild animals that people trapped. Today, about half comes from animals raised on ranches.

To make a fur coat, a furrier selects *pelts* —skins—that match in color and texture. The pelts are treated to make them flexible and durable. Then they are cleaned, sometimes dyed, and cut into small strips. The strips are sewed together into sections that make up the coat.

A fur coat is expensive because it uses pelts from many animals and requires so much handwork. But many people like to wear fur because of its warmth and beauty.

Some people think it is wrong to kill animals for their fur. Instead, people often wear artificial furs made from synthetic fibers.

furniture

People use furniture to make sleeping, eating, and sitting more comfortable. We also use furniture to store things. Furniture can be heavy and solid, or it can be lightweight and fold up. It is made from a variety of materials. Chairs, tables, beds, cabinets, and desks are a few examples of furniture.

Early people slept on beds of leaves or animal skins. They sat on rocks, fallen logs, blankets, or mats. This was their furniture. It had to be easy to carry or something that could be left behind when they traveled. Once people learned to raise crops, they were able to settle in one place. Their homes—and their furniture—became more permanent.

Stools, chairs, benches, tables, chests, and beds are the most useful pieces of furniture. So people built these first. They are shown in ancient Babylonian, Egyptian, and Greek art. Our knowledge of ancient furniture also comes from the pieces and models of furniture the Egyptians buried with their dead.

Furniture designs fit how people live. In Asia, where people sit on the floor or on cushions, tables are very low. The ancient Greeks and Romans lay down on low couches while they ate. In Europe during the

Changing styles:
chairs made in
the 1700s (below),
the 1800s
(far right),
and the
late 1900s
(right).

Middle Ages, common people sat together on benches or three-legged stools. Chairs were for the nobility or important guests. Castles were drafty, so the beds had drapes to keep out cold. In tropical areas, people sleep under a "mosquito net" to keep out insects.

Wood is the most common material for furniture. It can be cut and carved into intricate shapes. Benches and thrones have also been carved from stone. Clay can be molded into small tables and stools. Wicker furniture is woven from strong plant fibers or stems. The seat of a chair or the frame of a bed may be laced with ropes or with strips of leather or cloth. Cushions and couches are covered with cloth or leather. Today, plastic and metal are molded into furniture, too.

Most people want furniture that is attractive as well as useful. Some furniture is decorated with painted or carved designs. *Inlays* —small pieces of ivory, gold, wood, stones, or gems set into the surface—add color and pattern. Cloth may be embroidered or printed with pictures and designs. Plastic and painted furniture can be any color.

The Victorian room below has rich design and furnishings. The Japanese living room at right has a simpler design.

Today, most furniture is made in factories. But craftspeople still make furniture by hand. Some copy old designs. Others create new designs. A few designers use humor. They make beds that look like cars, or chairs that look like huge baseball mitts.

To meet certain needs, people have designed special-purpose furniture. A doctor's examining table, for example, is at a height comfortable for a doctor to examine a patient. A television stand with wheels makes it easy to move a heavy television. Another example of special-purpose furniture is a student's school desk. It is child-size, has a writing surface, a place for books and supplies, and often an attached seat.

See also **fashion.**